"A gripping account of a [...] ents for failure, but her i[...] to overcome. When God became the power in her life, there was no stopping her. As I wiped tears, I was also amazed and inspired by her courage."

Reverend Charles A. Hutchins, M.S.W.

"'Mama Rita,' that's my name for her. Having known her for less than one year, she has filled a void in my life after moving from my biological mother. After reading her book, it confirms her "Mama Rita" name to me. She has shown me strength and love and that God is the answer to all of life, and without him we are nothing. No matter what in life we may endure, we can overcome and fulfill our dreams and have our 'Happy House.'"

Christy Phillips,
Friend and Co-worker

"[*My Journey to My Happy House*]…so tenderly travels through… innocence it leaves me with such a vision of [the author] and [her] existence of loneliness, yet strength."

Trudy,
Friend

"In my eyes, my mother was and is a great person. As I read the issues that followed her life, I realize her favorite verse was indeed truth, 'When thy Father and thy Mother forsake thee the Lord will take thee up.' I have seen it with my own eyes, *God* took her up, for she had every reason to live a life of bitterness and anger. She chose to lean on God, but not before God chose to let her lean."

Synthia,
Daughter

# My Journey To My Happy House

# MY JOURNEY TO MY HAPPY HOUSE

rita sexton

TATE PUBLISHING & *Enterprises*

Published by Tate Publishing & Enterprises, LLC
127 E. Trade Center Terrace | Mustang, Oklahoma 73064 USA
1.888.361.9473 | www.tatepublishing.com

Tate Publishing is committed to excellence in the publishing industry. The company reflects the philosophy established by the founders, based on Psalm 68:11,
*"The Lord gave the word and great was the company of those who published it."*

Book design copyright © 2007 by Tate Publishing, LLC. All rights reserved.
*Cover design by Kellie Southerland*
*Interior design by Steven Jeffrey*

Published in the United States of America

ISBN: 978-1-60247-866-4
1. Christian Living: Practical Life   2. Nonfiction: Family & Relationships:
07.10.10

The amazing story of how God brought a little girl from
the depths of abuse to a life of joy.


"When my father and my mother forsake me, then the
Lord will take me up."
Psalms 27:10, KJV

# CONTENTS

# FOREWORD

I was honored when Rita asked me to help her write this story. Even though she lived with my family for two years and we have stayed in touch all of these years, there was much of her story that I did not know. I never realized the degree of pain she suffered as a child or in her first two marriages.

I knew the first time I saw Rita as a teenager that she had some very special qualities and that she deserved to have a life better than she had. The decision to take her into our home was never a difficult one. We had our home approved for foster care, and Rita lived with us as a "free foster child," meaning that we received no compensation for her care and that she was free to discontinue the relationship whenever she chose.

Both of our extended families and our children have always accepted her as part of our family. Now that she is happily married to Jim, he has embraced us as part of his family (a relationship we never enjoyed with either of her other husbands). We are so happy that she and Jim found each other and that their home is open to friends and family, neighbors, and their children's friends, and that all of them are serving the Lord. We give God praise and thankfulness for making this family a part of our lives and pray that we will always be a blessing to them.

Eva Grey Hutchins

# PREFACE

I have often been encouraged to tell my story, but I was reluctant to open my life to public scrutiny. Now I understand that by doing so I may help someone else to realize that no matter what their circumstances, they are not alone. Though I've thought I would like to forget the past, I look back and realize that I am now comfortable with myself and my life. Those events helped shape me into the person I have become. I share this story only because I want to glorify God for what He has done with someone who was abused as a child in every conceivable way, who experienced abandonment and neglect, pain, horror, and shame. I realize that I have risked a great deal in telling the whole story, but I pray that God can use my story to help someone know they are not going through life's struggles alone, and that the miracle of God's divine intervention can bring release, forgiveness, and wholeness. Perhaps opening my life on these pages will allow someone to be freed from bondage situations or relationships. My intent in telling this story is not to harm or hurt any of the people who have been a part of the story, but to bring glory to God, who redeemed me from a horrible situation and brought me new life. I praise Him that out of the experiences of my past He was able to keep me and to bring me at last to where I am today, with a loving family, a house full of joy, happiness and obedience to God.

# ACKNOWLEDGMENTS

Without the support of my beloved husband, Jim, I could not have told this story. He encouraged me, gave me strength, and has been willing to wait until I am finished to learn the details that I have been unable to share with him or anyone. He has loved me unconditionally and taught me how to love and trust him. I thank him always, as I thank God for bringing him into my life.

I thank my children: Heather, Holly, Brandon, and Synthia, for their unconditional love and forgiveness in spite of the years of pain they endured because of my fears and sinfulness. What a blessing it is to see them grow into Christ believing, born-again Christians, and what a difference that makes in raising children. My grandchildren are blessed to know and understand the Lord so early in their lives. I thank God for the blessings of my grandchildren. They, too, are special gifts; I am a blessed Nana of Logan, Lexi, Dylan, Megan, Noah, Victoria, Isabella, and Tanner, who we lost July 1995, to a stillborn birth. They are "sunshine" of my life and the absolute reflection of God's Almighty power to bring everything together for good. I now *know* I am loved. I also find such a blessing in the children that have come to me in the form of a beautiful package that my husband presented to me upon our marriage, my stepson, Jamie, and stepdaughter, Angie. Jamie is married to Nikisha; their children, who also bless our lives, are Christian, Breanna, and Morgan—Jamie's son from a pervious marriage. Angie has recently returned home after years with Com-Air serving as an airline attendant; God has some special plans for her.

I thank God for the love of my two brothers, Johnny and Vaughn, who went through many of these trials and tribulations along with me. They were the source of my strength for many of our young years. After all, they were my first babies.

I thank God that we have found our youngest brother, Michael. He, too, has seen tragedy and pain as a child of a mother whose heart was cold and uncaring. Thank God he was raised by a stepfather who taught him what love from a parent should be. Michael has two sons.

I thank God for many witnesses of hope in Christ. I see those much younger going through life alone but have found God to be the true source of their strength. I am reminded especially of Barbara Adkison Clendenon, who is absolutely amazing. Through trials and tribulation, she has chosen to be a Woman of Faith and a godly expression through her chosen walk to follow the God of Mercy and Grace. It is so fulfilling to see her building her own *"Happy House,"* along with her husband, Todd, and daughter, Madison.

I thank Charles and Eva Grey Hutchins, my foster parents, who guided me, counseled me, and have never let me go. Thanks, Mom Hutchins, for your invaluable help in putting this story together and for being that loving example of the unconditional love of a mother.

Thank you, Daddy Charles, for the love that you have shown by your nearly fifty years of unselfish giving to children who had no one else, most of them never knowing the loving hand you played in healing their little torn lives. Thank you to the sister and brothers who didn't have to be, Camille, Ralph, and John.

Most of all, I thank God for all the goodness and love He has showered upon me and for letting me know He was always there, through the good and bad times. He continues to redeem me and guide me in His ways.

"A Real Princess"

Angels watching over me
instructed by the God
who fashioned me before I knew,
I was even loved.

At times I felt discouraged,
I needed peace and rest,
then he'd cuddle my small face,
and hold me to his chest.

I wanted to feel special,
"a princess" wannabe,
I'd sit and think, then dream about
someone loving me.

Then in silence
a voice I heard
calling out my name,
it was a message from the God above,
I'd never be the same.

In that loving message,
the words they helped me see
My Father was the
"King of Kings,"
So what did that make Me?

*written by Rita Sexton*

# CHAPTER ONE

My understanding is, I was born to a nineteen-year-old woman named Ruby. She was married at a young age to my father, who was around age twenty-four at the time of my birth.

My life began rather strange for me. I was born in Washington, D.C., hundreds of miles away from my father and his home in Johnson City, Tennessee. I have been told my parents were estranged at that time.

I was brought home from the hospital to the house of Aunt Corey and her live-in boyfriend, Jesse. I was told that my mother, while in the hospital, named me "Beverly." A few weeks later, she changed my name to "Darlene." Then, because Jesse enjoyed the presence of a baby, gave her the idea I should be named after him. Now I was known as "Jessica"…but not for long! Apparently, my father came back into the picture shortly after my birth, (I know this because I have a brother who is twelve months and ten days younger than me) I was renamed after my father. I was called "Billie Lee."

The strangest part of this whole naming situation is that some four years later during my adoption proceeding, it was found that I had no name. My birth certificate was void of a full birth name.

Some time after the birth of my brother Johnny, conflicts escalated between our father and mother. I never learned exactly why, but I have my suspicions, which are detailed in the next few paragraphs. Our father went to Florida in search of a job. After he left, Ruby sold everything in the house, piled Father's clothes in the middle of the floor, and left. By the time he returned, we were gone. I was always told she didn't leave town alone, but purportedly in the company of a professor from a nearby college, whom she had been seeing. Shortly thereafter, Ruby apparently learned she was pregnant again. At what point my brother Vaughn was born, I am uncertain, but it is certain that he was born in Johnson City, Tennessee, per his birth certificate, although family members said they were unaware of his existence until we were reunited with our father some eight years later. Whether Vaughn was a surprise or not, whether he belonged to our dad or not, is irrelevant to us. We have a bond, and we all belong to each other.

Family have said that our dad adored me and I adored him. He was the typical alcoholic, coming home, passing out wherever he fell. He had a nasty demeanor when under the influence of alcohol, always trying to pick fights with anyone—family, strangers, the neighbors walking the dog—but was always good to me or as good as a drunk can be. He must have had a lot of pent-up aggressions; although, I understand that when he was sober, he was a kind man. Alcohol brought out the worst in him. His sisters and brothers told me that he grieved for years over the loss of his children. It would be more than eight years before we would see him again.

# CHAPTER TWO

Fragmented memories are all that serve me from this point to our adoption because there is no one who can verify or share anything.

Brother Johnny and I, in the same crib, wake up to see something we had not witnessed before—our mother in bed with someone other than our father. We must have been staying in a one-bedroom house or apartment. I remember her noticing me and saying, "How would you like to have a new little brother?" to which I recall giggling. I could not have been much more than two. Some say this was impossible, but although there is no one to verify it as I have grown, it still is as vivid as the day those words were spoken. I do believe traumatic events stimulate long-term memory. I realize just the fact she mentioned a baby brother is strange because that's exactly what she had. She named him Vaughn.

Living in a two-bedroom apartment. Johnny and I sleeping on a couch with protruding springs, around which we learned to curl our bodies so as not to lay on them. I remember knowing I had to keep my arms very close to me for fear the mice we heard at night would bite us if our arms fell off the couch. We had no coverings but slept only in whatever we wore to bed, which most of the time was what we had worn that day. Vaughn had a crib. There was no other furniture in the room—just the crib against the wall and the couch in the middle of the floor. Dad was not a part of our lives at this time.

Mother had been gone a long, long time, from "one-night-time to another-night-time" is how I explained her absence to a questioning neighbor after I had opened the front door to ask her if she had seen my mother.

How hungry we were! The baby was crying and we all were starving. I looked in the refrigerator; there was no more canned spaghetti. Mother kept opened cans of spaghetti in the refrigerator, which we ate directly from the can with our fingers. She didn't like being bothered when we became hungry. Same day, opening the front door, smelling the odor of food. Someone was cooking. I followed the smell. I came to an apartment, which I remember being underground with concrete steps going down to it. I crept down the steps. The door was open, but the screen door was closed. I looked in no one was there. I looked directly into the kitchen and saw food on the stove. I was *so* hungry! I spied a loaf of bread on the kitchen table. I quietly opened the door, quietly closed it, and ran as fast as I could to grab that loaf of bread for us. I got to the door, threw it open, and sprinted up the short row of steps as I heard the door slam behind me. In my very young mind, I believed that someone had caught me and was after me. I ran even faster. Alas, a criminal at age three and a half! But I was able to feed my hungry brothers that evening.

Mother coming home and shortly thereafter was visited by a woman with a black briefcase. Later I realized it was a caseworker from the Human Services Department who had come either because my neighbor contacted them when I told her my mother was absent or because the family from which I stole the loaf of bread actually saw my getaway. I was later told the caseworker had given Mother two weeks to straighten up her life or we were going to be removed. Mother was not going to let anyone tell her what she could or could not do, so she chose to look for her own way out.

I awakened one morning to find my little brother missing. I remember crying, "My baby! My baby!" I remember that Mother showed no concern. Although I was only three and a half years old, some forty years later I can still feel the pain in my chest, which now I relate to missing someone, almost as in death. I loved my brothers. Later I found that Mother had given Vaughn to a friend named Daisy, who was as poor a mother as ours. Daisy was also an acquaintance of the couple who would later adopt us. This is how they came to know about us. We were advertised like used cars for sale.

Still crying and looking for my baby brother. A couple of strangers came to visit one evening. I recall intensely listening to them but didn't quite understand why they were there. I learned all too quickly they had come to take Johnny and me away. I hid under a chair in the living room, crawling under the back of it while the skirt around it covered my hiding place. I laid there believing they would leave without me because they couldn't see me.

Suddenly, after several calls yielded no cooperation from me, the chair was lifted off of me. I was taken gently by the arm and was told I was going with them. Being led away, I recall looking back at my mother. I distinctly remember that she never looked at us. I remember calling to her, but just as though we didn't exist she continued what she was doing never looking up. Later I was told that she had asked them to complete the transaction as soon as possible, as she had a date and didn't want to be late for it. No matter how cruel a mother may be, a small child loves her unconditionally for one reason: they have nothing to compare their mother to, therefore it is total unconditional love and trust. Whatever she was, whatever she did was just normal to us. She was our mother and we loved her, but unfortunately just because we were her children didn't give her cause for those same feelings.

That night was so traumatic. I remember everything about it- even to the way my mother wore her hair, how she was dressed, the way she sat on the couch, where she sat on the couch in relation to where the visitors sat, the way the room was laid out, where each piece of furniture was placed, and where the refrigerator was.

That same night we were led to a car, and I was urged into the backseat with Johnny, the two of us sitting quietly as if someone had just kidnapped us. I remember being the protector. I leaned forward and said, "It's okay to take us tonight, but my mommy wants us back tomorrow!" The "stranger" spoke words that ripped my tiny heart, "No, dear, your mother doesn't ever want you back." Tears immediately flooded my eyes, holding Johnny and burying my face into his arm, inserting my thumb into my mouth, and silently crying myself to sleep. I don't recall Johnny crying at all. This memory is one of the three most vivid of all.

The lady must have been telling the truth, because our mother never came for us, although we watched for her daily. Eventually, the pain of wanting her became less; then she became a memory, and when that happened, she moved out of our hearts. Little Vaughn was still gone, and I still cried for him everyday and especially at night. He never moved out of our hearts.

Our lives were very different in our new home. We had clean beds. We shared a room, but it was unlike what we shared before—no protruding springs and plenty of covers. We also had plenty of food, very nice clothes. But I still missed my brother, "my baby."

I recall that I got in trouble a lot for hiding food, sometimes between my thighs in the chair, sometimes in pockets on my clothes. I couldn't believe that I didn't have to ever worry about eating again. I was assured that there would always be food, and there was!

I remember being with a babysitter one day, when she said to me, "Come, look outside!" I went running. The family car had just pulled up; our new parents got out, walked to the back door of the driver's side of the car, and opened it; a set of baby feet hit the ground. I must have looked puzzled, but just for a moment, because when the owner of those two feet came into view, it was "my baby." I remember screaming and running out the door then grabbing him around the neck, crying, "My baby! My baby!" Life just became the best. Vaughn, Johnny, and I were all together again. This is number two of the three most vivid memories.

# CHAPTER THREE

It took a long time for us to trust our new parents. We had been programmed to believe that "daddy" was a bad word. Whenever we questioned our birth mother about where our dad was, she always made certain that we knew our dad was a "bad" man and that we should not ask about him.

We had lived in our new home for about six months, and I recall going to what I now know was a court hearing. I was called to sit near the judge, and he proceeded to ask me questions. I only recall one question, and that was "the question": Would you want to live with your mother, or would you rather live with your new parents?" I remember very vividly-the deep, depressing, chest-crushing, almost smothering hurt—but also a hopeful feeling as my heart raced. I was hoping to see my mother. As I looked around the courtroom, packed (so it seemed) with people, I knew if I saw her I would tell her how much I wanted to be with her. Words cannot express how much I wanted her to be there…but she wasn't. I looked around one more time. My eyes filled with tears, I had to keep blinking to be able to see people's faces. No Mother, so I said, "With my new parents." Until I die, I will always remember the pain of that day and looking through tears. This is number three of my three most vivid memories.

This four-year-old finally had a name, Rita Ann—Rita coming from my adopted father's favorite movie star, Rita Hayworth. He showed me a picture of her and asked if it would be okay to be named after her. I remember thinking, *She is so pretty, and maybe if I have her name, I will grow up to be pretty*. Ann came from his mother. That felt special.

My sweet brothers kept their names They, too, were named after other well-known personalities of that era. My biological father, being a country and western music buff, named Johnny after Johnny Cash, and my biological mother named Vaughn after Vaughn Monroe, also a country and western legend, singer and "Big band leader." Neither of them ever hoped to look like or be like their namesake.

Our new family was military, so shortly after we became an official family, our new dad was sent overseas and we followed soon thereafter. Sorrento, Italy, became our new home. After thirteen days aboard a large ocean liner, we stepped onto a land that was to be our home for the next three and a half years.

Our home was on the third floor of an apartment complex. It had marble floors and a living room with French doors that opened up to a most beautiful view of the Mediterranean Sea. Although the apartment was very modest, it was a clean and warm home.

Soon after moving to Italy, I began having nightmares so devastating that professional counseling was sought. Horrifying events from my past I had suppressed began to surface. The counselor uncovered as a very small child, my mother often left me with a neighbor, a man I called "Grandpa Washington." He was an African-American who repeatedly molested me. I was too young to understand the situation was wrong but had enough understanding to be scared. It took nearly two years to completely get over the nightmares.

Even though life was better, something was still lurking around, trying to destroy the security I had finally found. I remember distinctly seeing visions behind the door in my room. I would start to shut the door, and "it" was standing there, not moving. "It" was dressed in something similar to a monk's attire, black robe with a huge hood, big sleeves, skirt all the way to the floor, and a rope tied around "its" middle. Somehow I related "it" to the male gender. The space under the hood where a face should be was nothing but darkness. The sleeves were held at the waist, giving me the impression that the arms were held by one another. "It" exposed nothing human except form. This only happened in my bedroom, behind my door. I never told anyone. This continued to happen for years, and as quickly as it appeared, it dissipated. Sometime, after we had moved from Italy to Key West, Florida, "its" visits ceased. I was about nine years old.

* * *

I started kindergarten in an Italian Catholic school. It was very different, but I learned to speak the language quickly. I remember the first day. I stood with my mother at the bus stop, thinking we were going together, the bus stopped, Mother helped me step up and said to find a seat. I took a seat, looked out the window, mother was still standing there. I started crying. I immediately thought I was being taken away again. It was an extremely traumatic event. That afternoon the bus brought me back to the same bus stop, where she and my brothers were waiting for me.

I vividly recall missing the after-school bus one afternoon. I was walking towards the bus and noticed a piece of chewing gum stuck to the sidewalk. (We never got candy or gum, but I knew what it was). I didn't worry about germs; I just wanted the gum. I pulled and yanked, pulled and yanked until finally it broke loose, I popped it in my mouth. As I was savoring the flavor (what was left), I realized the bus had just left. I stood and watched it go out of sight. I walked around and didn't know what to do. Although I was very scared, I started to walk home. I was familiar with the route. I noticed the janitor watching me, as he had done on other days, mostly in the halls from his janitorial closet or while I was at lunch. I had a built-in alarm system regarding strange men, and it was going off. He showed concern for my predicament, but I was still afraid. He didn't touch me but acted as though he was guiding me to someone who could help me. I reluctantly followed. Of course, I didn't understand what he was saying because he spoke fluent Italian, and at that time I didn't. When we got to a place, a remote side of the building, he grabbed me by the arm and dragged me to a tall patch of bushes. I screamed, kicked, and fought and somehow got away from him. I ran all the way home, where my mother was frantic. Even with what I had been through, I still had that gum in my mouth. She made me spit it out. She had no idea what I had gone through for that piece of gum. If I still had it today, it would be framed! I got a scolding and a spanking. I never told her about the janitor, nor do I recall ever being bothered by or ever seeing him again. I was never late for the school bus again.

I also remember while in Sorrento, my mother received a telegram that her mother had passed away. She lay on her bed, cried a while, got up, and never mentioned it again. She didn't attempt to go to the funeral.

We had many unique friends. My best friend was Amelia, she was the niece of our maid, Maria. Amelia had lost her parents in a car accident and Maria was raising her. We had so much fun together. We'd play on the high hill behind my home. I especially remember her teaching me that you could hold onto the tail of lizards and they would wiggle until they would detach their bodies from their own tails. Wow! She assured me they would grow another one. That became a daily routine. I hope it wasn't cruel. I didn't want to be cruel.

Years later when we returned to the States, I always believed I would see her again, however that never happened. I often think about her still.

Our dad was in the navy and spent a lot of time at sea; sometimes he was gone for six weeks or more at a time. We really liked it when he was home because he was the loving, nurturing one. He gave us a lot of hugs and kisses, and he loved to cook. Mother, on the other hand, was extremely clean, wanted no messes, she was very, *very* strict. Children were expected to have good manners at all times, to a degree that was painful. "Manners" included shaking hands with adults, which always got a smile or a laugh. We were to be seen and not heard, the perfect specimens of dwarf adults. She constantly received compliments, and we were her achievements. As an adult, I am grateful for much of her parenting, but as children we missed a lot of "normal childhood." It would have been nice just to have been children.

Around my sixth birthday, Mother took me to ballet lessons. She soon removed me, however, as I was doing my own dancing and not listening to each important step. I was intrigued with the older girls and what they were doing. I would run to the stretch bar and try to hike my leg up to follow what they were doing. They'd soon be relieved of my presence, as someone would come, grab me by the arm and take me back to that place I found to be baby stuff. It quickly became apparent that I was not interested in dancing and was very bored with the fundamentals of dance classes.

I was also a girl who had a real baby, Vaughn. So when I got dolls with moving parts, I took them apart to see how they did what they did. Finally, with my mother's desire for me to have a girlie room like other girls my age, she would buy "don't touch" dolls that would just sit on my bed. I remember them being almost the same size as me. I was told that the only time I was to touch them was to take them off the bed so I could sleep then to put them back on the bed after I made it up. I was afraid to disobey her.

We all made our beds, even at the young ages of four and five. Mother was a stickler for perfection. When we made our beds, she'd better not see any wrinkles under the bedspread or she'd jerk the linens off the bed and we would have to do it again. You knew she was satisfied when you could bounce a coin off it. If the coin didn't bounce, off came the sheets and bedspread and you began again.

Mother was determined to "make something" out of me. She bought me a guitar, and every Saturday morning we would board first a bus, then a train into Naples. There we visited a gentleman who gave private guitar lessons. Patiently, while occasionally dashing to his cabinet for some aspirin, he taught me the Spanish guitar, I became very good. Later, I found that he was a very renowned composer. That was special. However, I really wasn't interested or committed to learning to play a guitar by age eight. After much pushing and prodding, she gave up, and I laid my instrument down. Occasionally, I would pick it up, but since I had never seen a girl play a guitar, I decided it was something only boys did. I do wish I had continued.

The early years with our adoptive parents were good in many respects. There were a lot of rules, strictly enforced by Mother. Dad, on the other hand, was compassionate and caring. He would take time to talk with us, and when we were hurting, he always came to our rooms to talk about it. We always felt that he shared a lot of wisdom with us. We found love in him, the kind we needed to survive.

Dad was raised in North Carolina as a Baptist. Mother grew up in Pawtucket, Rhode Island, as a Catholic. I don't recall going to church often, for they were not faithful members. We attended the Episcopal church on rare occasions. That seemed to be a compromise. It didn't matter, though, because it didn't last long. I recall going with Mother once or twice to a Catholic church where she lit candles and prayed. I believe it was for her daughter-in-law, who was ill and eventually died.

After moving from Sorrento, we spent a time in Norfolk, Virginia, before being transferred to Key West, Florida. There, while I was in the third grade, my mother shared with me a strange conversation. She stated I was old enough to hear some things that had happened in her life. Of course, I was all ears, but what I heard disturbed me; I realize now, I was too young to hear. She told me that as a teenager she had been raped, as a result of that rape, she had a son, whom she named Tony. Her mother raised the child for her because our mother said she couldn't. Our adopted mother eventually married a Mr. Spence; he must have been the love of her life. Even as young as I was I could see every time she spoke of him, her eyes were distant. She said he adopted Tony, and together they were raising him in a real family. Eventually, Mr. Spence went to war, was killed and buried somewhere in Europe.

Tony ended back with his grandmother, and our mother went on with her life. Eventually, she married again to a Mr. Tad. That marriage didn't last long because she said it was abusive. On September 22, 1955, they divorced. She then met and married a military naval man who would become our adoptive dad. They married July 5, 1956; this information was found in her belongings upon her death.

Mother often told me that her mother did not like her. She was the only girl of four children. She and her brothers were not close; we never knew why, although on occasion she tried to find them. I don't recall she was ever successful in reaching them.

Although she was very rigid with us regarding decency, morality, and all that goes with that, she apparently did not always mirror those images. Pictures found after her death among her belongings depicted a very different lifestyle. Some pictures showed her in bars, drinking, smoking, and flirting with men. Some pictures portrayed her as seductive, strangely different than from the woman we had come to know.

I knew fairly early I was not loved extremely or even moderately by our adoptive mother, much like she was treated by her mother. I loved styling my hair, but she always kept it cut short after I got older, except a few times that I was allowed to let it grow. When I was about ten, I recall standing in front of the mirror and fixing my hair in a bun on top of my head. We had guests who walked past my bedroom door and said, "How does she do that? It looks so cute." It was a compliment that made me feel good. That evening after the company left, she sat me down, threw a towel around my neck, and cut my hair into a "pixie." I sat there and cried. I didn't understand. I also remember going to school the next day wanting to fade into the wall. I felt I was being stared and laughed at, while everyone kept asking, "What happened to your hair?" The giggles were damaging.

Another time I remember our parents asking us what we wanted for Christmas. Johnny and Vaughn eagerly told what they wanted, and I remember saying, "White boots with heels." It was the big Nancy Sinatra era, and she had just recorded "These Boots Were Made for Walking." I yearned for a pair of white boots with heels. The boots were all I asked for. Under the tree several weeks later, I saw a boot box wrapped up. Oh, I was excited! Christmas morning came. I couldn't wait. The box was handed to me. I ripped through the wrapping and opened the box. Sadness hit. I was given a pair of white vinyl boots with flat heels. They were nothing like I imagined, nothing like Nancy's. Seeing my ingratitude, Mother said I was lucky to get anything. The boots I wanted were too expensive. I went to my room and cried. Dad came in to console me; he made the gift acceptable to me.

We visited Mother's son Tony on the occasion of his wife's severe illness. The illness ended in her eventual death due to complications in childbirth. It was her eighth pregnancy. I can recall Mother talking about what a "pigsty" Tony's house was and how she couldn't believe people lived like that. I distinctly remember thinking how sick Tony's wife was and how sad it was Mother was talking about her, especially while Tony's wife couldn't do anything about it.

I can remember wondering why our mother did not share more time with Tony and his family. We had never been there before and they had never visited us. In reality, I don't think she was much more of a mother to him than our biological mother was to us. In a time of crisis, though, she did respond, but I'm not sure what benefit we were, if any. We stayed a while, long enough to go to school with his children for several weeks and to meet Tony's new girlfriend.

It was an unusual time. I recall knowing before the children that their mother had died but being told not to tell. I'm ashamed to say I told one the girls. I'm not sure if it was because I knew something no one else knew, which made me feel powerful, or because I had already been through so much personally that I was oblivious to the pain it might cause. Maybe I was curious to see her reaction. I had no real reason for doing it, but it was wrong. She never let on she already knew when they broke the news to them. I still think about that.

After that, I became the protector of Tony's children. I got in trouble more than once for taking up for the children when the bullies would come around. There was a gang of them. Tony had a very hard time just feeding a family of that size. The low-rent housing complex was all he could afford. There were always bullish children trying to cause trouble and fights, trying to make their mark—most of the time, the mark they wanted to make was on other children.

Days after their mother's funeral, we were all outside playing when a couple of those neighborhood bullies came around and started teasing them, calling them orphans and motherless, to which I came out swinging and swinging and I swung some more. I hit one or two, was hit back, but was so mad I didn't feel it. I just wanted to shut them up. It worked. Then I was punished and put in a bedroom for the rest of the afternoon because, as Mother said, "Girls don't act like that!" As I sat in that room alone, I had to smile because outside I could hear my brothers and all of Tony's older children yelling at the bullies, "She won; she beat you up! Bet you'll leave us alone now. She knocked your heads off and she's a girl!" That made it all worth it. "The Terminator" was born in me that day.

We finally left Tony's home and returned to our residence in Norfolk. We had not seen our dad in about a month, we were happy to be near him again. He knew how to cook really well. He fixed our supper that night. For dessert he made homemade donuts. We thought he could do anything and everything.

I remember around age ten, I often thought about all the children in the world who were without a mother to love and care about them. That struck a chord with me because of my past. I formed a club called "The Helpful Hands" and tried to contact businesses and civic clubs, with Mother's help and the help of other girls from school and my brothers. We solicited money to benefit children who needed care. Of course, I insisted that my brothers also become involved in our project. We met every Monday. I even wrote a song. I could still play the guitar well enough to strum the tune "Santa Lucia," to which we sang our song "We are the Helpful Hands." We were able to raise about $120. Mother told us it would be nice to send it to Tony, since he was having such a hard time. Everyone agreed. A reporter from the local newspaper came out and did a story that winter. We were celebrities! Or so we thought.

The next several months were filled with visiting groups to solicit money for The Helpful Hands. It felt wonderful to do something for children who were suffering. The scars from our early childhood, although years past, still left a painful imprint. This opportunity helped us to feel that we were doing something special for someone else.

I recall Johnny having a difficult time in school. Mother was less than understanding. She would sit him at the table with a book between his hands. (Again, I remind you that nothing but perfection was acceptable to her.) Every night he would read, with every mispronounced word she would take a ruler and whack his knuckles. The strike would crack as though his knuckles were shattering. He would sit there crying, unable to hold the hand that was hurting because she wouldn't allow him to move it. I would hide my face in my pillow while I covered my ears. He would cry, I would cry, I hated her for treating him that way. He would be so afraid of making a mistake that he would make more. I would sit in my room adjacent to the kitchen where he was, trying tele-pathically to help him (though I didn't realize that's what I was doing). Of course, it didn't help him.

That was also the year he had to repeat a grade. I was so angry with his teacher. I paced the floor outside her door, thinking of the right thing to say to make her feel bad about what she had done to him. I must have walked it off, I left without saying anything. I was still my brother's protector.

I fought more fights for Johnny. If he came home bloody or bruised, I'd go after the culprits, regardless of how many or how big. The anger in me for what they had done to him fueled me enough to wipe out half the block by myself. I don't ever remember losing. I was the feared female on the block when it came to my brothers. As I look back, I wonder if some of those fights were encouraged by Johnny just to see me take up for him.

Johnny still talks about one fight he was involved in when my friend and I approached.

"What's going on, Johnny?" I asked.

He replied, "I'm trying to fight these boys. They've been teasing me and won't leave me alone."

He still laughs at my response. As I began rolling up my sleeves, I said, "Take a break." I started punching. He claims when I was done, none were left standing. The Terminator had struck again.

At age eleven, my whole world turned upside down and ended in torment. My parents, who never drank, at least not in our pres-ence, decided to have a New Year's Eve party at our house. They sent us to bed. I don't remember hearing a thing until someone awakened me, his hands in places that I knew were forbidden. With my heart racing and my tears suppressed, I began pushing away the hands that were violating me. The odor that reeked from his breath was unfamiliar, but the voice spoken from the mouth pressed tightly against my face was. I shuddered with disgust. It was my dad, the man I adored, the one person I had grown to love and trust more than anyone else except my brothers. His words to me were, "If you scream, I'll slap your face!" Even though the voice sounded like my dad, it wasn't my dad talking. My dad protected me; he would never hurt me. I struggled, but he forcefully said, "Lie still and be quiet, or I'll put my hand over your mouth." I began to cry as quietly as I could, in a loud whisper he said sternly, "Shut up, or I'll stuff your mouth with a sock!" My wonderful world with my wonderful Dad had vanished. Things would never be the same. That night I lost decency, love, trust, security, and my dad. That unfamiliar odor I now know was alcohol.

I became a recluse in my room when I wasn't at school or doing my chores at home. I never went out anymore to play; I never went to visit my friend. I was afraid all over again. I had lost my Dad, the one adult I fully trusted and adored.

Mother noticed the change in my behavior, Dad confessed. She came to me and asked me why I hadn't told her, while in the same breath asked if I had told anyone else. I didn't know why I had not told her, and no, I hadn't told anyone, I responded. She insisted that I not breathe a word to anyone, and I didn't.

Shortly thereafter, she took me to see a doctor. She told me the reason was I had not started my womanly cycle, and she wanted to know if there was a problem. I was only eleven. An internal exam was performed. I felt humiliated, but I believed her. Years later, I realized she was having me checked because of what had happened to me. Later I was told the doctor had been lead to believe I was a young girl with a wild side.

On the way home from the doctor's office, I began to have difficulty breathing. I've had recurrences of that experience through the years, a condition I now recognize as anxiety or panic attack. Mother assured me it was nothing, which only made it worse because I knew it was something. I always thought I was dying because I could not breathe. Over time I've learned how to control those attacks.

I remember one of the worst attacks I ever had came after she confronted me about the horrible experience of that night. What she didn't realize was it wasn't just that night. The abuse had continued. Her reasoning for the incident was I pranced around in my nightgown in front of my dad and teased him. I was only eleven. I didn't understand what she meant. He was my dad, not once did I ever think of my dad or anyone else that way.

Another incident I recall during this dark time in my life was lying in bed and hearing a voice outside my window. I remember pulling up the covers over my head and feeling very threatened by the unknown. Eventually, I pulled the covers down to expose just my eyes, again I heard it. I covered my head again. I didn't dare cry because whoever or whatever was lurking outside my window might hear me and come in. The voice was a deep, devilish male voice. When I mustered enough courage to get up, I ran into my brothers' room and told them. There was a door between our rooms that was never opened. My dresser sat in front of it. We opened it and talked back and forth until I went to sleep. I don't recall hearing that voice again in the short time we had left in that house.

I began questioning, "Why? Why am I here?" I can even remember thinking, "*If this is all there is, you just live until you die, I want to die right now and get it over with.*" I remember, with the exception of going to church on holidays, praying that child's prayer once in a while, "Now I lay me down to sleep . . ." and going to confirmation class for my age every so often, God was never experienced in our home. However, there was a statue about eighteen inches high that sat on the chest of drawers in my room. It was a statue of Jesus. I remember touching his feet and holding his hand, rubbing my fingers over the nail scars. I was in awe of it. He was holding out his hands with the nail prints as if to say to me, "Come here to me." I would stare at the statue for long intervals of time. Somehow I knew he meant something, and that something was good.

Children not only get their feelings of self-worth from the way parents make them feel, but parents also give a glimpse of what God is, my glimpse so far was not a loving one. When I thought of God, I saw a stern, judgmental, less-than-loving being. Neither my adoptive parents nor my birth parents had given me any other image of God. Even if my adoptive father painted a picture of a loving God through his earlier actions, they certainly changed to dark and confusing because of his latter actions.

Whenever Mother was angry with me (which was often), she threatened, "You're going to grow up to be like Ruby." I always heard how terrible Ruby was; that was the most degrading thing she could have possibly said to me. I realize that we all have traits like our parents, some good, some bad, but I was always being told of how really, really bad she was, to be told I was going to be just like her was very damaging to me. Now, I was hearing it daily. My adopted mother would also state that she herself had never lied. "I hate liars," she'd say, hinting, of course, I was not truthful. That statement usually followed her discovery of something I had tried to conceal from her. For instance, she didn't allow me to wear make-up, but while at a friend's house we put on mascara, I forgot to wash it off. As soon as I walked in the door, she yelled, "What do you have on your eyes?" All I could see was the fire in her eyes, and I replied, "Nothing!" She took me to the bathroom and scrubbed my eyes with a soapy washcloth. I had fibbed to keep from getting a whipping, but I got the whipping and more.

Another time I was reminded of my heritage was after one Halloween night when my brothers and I came home with a very large stash of candy. When we got home, we were allowed to take out two pieces; the rest was put in a bowl and placed on top of the refrigerator—forever! She didn't allow us to have candy, but she loved it. One day as I was cleaning the kitchen after supper, I kept noticing that bowl with all that trapped, wrapped candy, enticing me to let it out. She would let us have Cracker Jacks, so I remembered an empty Cracker Jacks box in my lunch pail. I got it, while first making sure she was involved in her television show, I climbed up on a chair, got the bowl down, stuffed the Cracker Jacks box full, closed the lid on the bowl, and put it back in place. I was in candy heaven! I filled my mouth, closed the top of the box, and hid it behind my dresser.

The next day at school, all day long I thought about my box of candy. I couldn't wait to get home. Finally, the bell rang and school was over. I didn't wait on my brothers. I ran all the way home, burst through the front door, there was Mother in her usual position, watching television. "Hi, Mother. I'm home," I said as I ran to my room. Entering the room, what I saw dashed me with fear. My dresser was pulled away from the wall; the Cracker Jacks box was sitting on top. I ran over and grabbed it. All the candy was gone. She had found it. How did she know? Part of my discipline was to be reminded I was going to grow up to be like Ruby.

I recall another time I ended up in smoke...so to say! One day at Mary Calcott Elementary School, we had a bathroom break. As I entered the bathroom, a girl named Virginia was about to light a cigarette. We were all watching, thinking she was *so cool*. Virginia was really tall and a few years older than us, so naturally we all looked up to her. As she put the match to her cigarette, the bathroom door flew open and we heard the clinking of heels, which meant *teacher*! Virginia grabbed my purse and not only put her cigarette in it, *but the whole pack*! Everyone dashed around the teacher, who seemed to know that something was happening, of course, we all acted innocent. Virginia leaned over and said, "I'll get them after school."

Feeling a part of this adventure, I said, "Sure." What I forgot was that Mother was picking me up to go to the dentist right after school.

The dentist found I had three cavities. I would have opted for three more to have missed what I knew was about to take place. I held on to the purse as though it was my life. Mother started to take it while I was in the dentist's chair, but I quickly yanked it back. I could see that Mother's suspicion grew. When we got home, she demanded, "Let me see your purse!" If I had been a cussing kid, under my breath I would have said some big words. My eyes got big, *she knew*. "Let me see your purse," she said. I was frozen, so she took it. She opened it and asked, "Are these mine?"

Great! They were the same brand as hers; I immediately realized she was thinking I had taken hers. "No, they're someone else's," I said.

"Whose?" she asked.

I knew better than to tell because she would call Virginia's mother then the school. "They belong to a girl who put them in my purse in the bathroom because a teacher walked in," I responded with knees shaking like I was doing the twist.

"What's her name?" she calmly asked again.

"I don't know her name. She's not in my grade, but she's real tall," I said, hoping that would satisfy her.

She paused, then said, "Go take a bath."

Whew! I was glad that was over. Then fear hit me again. What was I going to tell Virginia the next day when she asked for her cigarettes?

I was in an awful predicament, but not like the one that was going to greet me upon completion of my bath. If I had known about what was to come, I might have considered drowning. Bathed and dressed, I came through the living room, into the kitchen, and headed for my bedroom. The only thing I was worried about was facing Virginia. I wasn't going to waste my time thinking about that today. However, before I could get to my room, my eyes turned to Mother sitting at the kitchen table. Supper wasn't on it, but that pack of cigarettes was, spread out with a pack of matches. There she sat, tapping her finger towards the chair opposite her. I couldn't read sign language, but I could read hers. I sat down. She told me to put a cigarette in my mouth and light it up. *You've got to be kidding*, I thought. She saw my concern and said, "Do it now! I've got to start supper; I want you to smoke this pack before supper."

So I began. I knew which end went in your mouth, but that's about all. I couldn't get it lit, so she told me how. "Take a deep breath as you bring the lighted match to the cigarette." I did, I thought I was going to choke to death coughing. It was not fun. But I got it lit.

"Smoke it," she said, I mocked what I had seen her do.

Evidently I wasn't doing it right, because she immediately stopped me to tell me the correct way. As I took a deep breath and drew from the cigarette, I began feeling lightheaded and very sick. I could feel my face turning green. I recall feeling so sick I just wanted to lay my head down, but she wouldn't allow that. Whenever I had the chance to puff instead of inhale, I would. Occasionally, she would leave the room or the phone would ring,

I took full advantage. After what seemed to me an eternity, the cigarettes were gone. I didn't eat supper that night! As if that were not punishment enough, I had to hear the lecture about growing up to be like Ruby and the threat of reform school. For years after that, just the thought of a cigarette or the smell of one brought me back to that experience, I'd become nauseated.

A few weeks later, she met me at the door as I came in from school. "I hope you had a good time at school today with your friends," she said, "because that will be the last time you'll see them."

"Are we moving again?" I asked.

"No, *we're* not going anywhere. Just you!" she responded.

"Oh?" I said, tears welling up in my eyes. "Where am I going?"

"Back to your family in Tennessee," she said. "I found your dad." Her voice was cold and bitter, and I surely felt the chill.

"Does he want us?" I asked.

"He'd better, because that's where you're headed," she responded. (I later learned that Mother had placed an ad in the Johnson City, Tennessee newspaper to locate my biological father.)

I couldn't tell a soul, not even my best friend, Debbie. But no sooner than I heard it, my brothers and I were on our way back to Tennessee. Just recently, some forty years later, my brother Vaughn shared with me that I was the only one who was supposed to leave home. He and Johnny were supposed to go back with them to Virginia, but the boys didn't want to leave me alone. I love my brothers.

# CHAPTER FOUR

Upon returning to Johnson City and the home of my biological father and his wife, Sharon, we were treated like a new car.

"Look, can you believe it? They've grown so much. Call Aunt Molly and Uncle Tom and tell 'em to come over. They'll never believe it!"

We were paraded around, hugged, stroked, kissed, and had to listen to stories that were so far-fetched we couldn't believe most of what we heard, much less understood. People came and went—like a funeral home on visitation night.

We spent hours and hours in that setting. Then it was time for our adopted parents to leave. I recall watching through the curtains in the living room of my grandparent's home. The thing I remember most is they never said goodbye, but my brothers were left with me and that made everything okay.

We soon moved into a two-bedroom apartment with my real Dad and Sharon. The day after we arrived, she told me, "I have a friend, but your daddy doesn't like him, so he visits me when your dad's at work. I expect you to keep it our secret." I agreed not to say anything. Of all the things that happened to me, I had never experienced anything like that before, but I'd had good practice in keeping secrets.

That afternoon, her "friend" came to visit. Sharon sent me and my brothers outside with our two-year-old half-brother and a stepbrother who was about seven. I began to realize there was something going on inside that was more than a visit between "friends." But I kept my word, even though I felt bad about it.

My biological dad had a number of sisters and several brothers. He was the youngest boy, and his sister Leah was the youngest of all. She was fun. I really liked her. She paid a great deal of attention to me, did my hair, bought make-up for me and at times just spent time with me. I really needed that. One day she took me on a date. At first, I thought that was cool. She took me behind a building where two African-American males waited in a car.

Upon entering the car, she gently pushed me away from the front car door and pointed to the backseat, where one man sat grinning and patting the seat. I remember looking at her with "please-don't-do-this-to-me" eyes, and she responded by whispering, "I won't let him hurt you."

I crawled in and hugged my door. Immediately, she was all over "her" guy, as he made a dive for her. I was speechless with surprise, especially when the man in the backseat grabbed my hand and tried to pull me his way. I pulled away and he dove for me. He held me down and started kissing my face while I squirmed. Where I got the strength I have no idea, but I managed to shove his face away and grab the door handle and got out. I opened the front door and jumped in the front seat, demanding to go home right then. Nothing I said, nothing I did took precedence over the state of mind Leah was in. I sat for the next thirty minutes witnessing things I should have never seen, while the pervert in the backseat did everything but crawl over the front seat with us. Needless to say, I never went back to Aunt Leah's house again, nor did I ever want to spend time with her.

The family of our stepmother, Sharon, lived in an isolated house in the mountains near Butler, North Carolina. We visited there frequently. There was no running water, no inside plumbing, no heat except for a pot-bellied stove that sat in the living room and served to heat the whole house—two bedrooms, a living room, and a kitchen. A wood stove was used to cook, and one large aluminum bucket served as drinking water for everyone. The water came from a spring. There was the absence of a driveway up to the house because the hill was too steep. We drove as close to the house as we could, then parked and walked the remaining half mile straight up.

When Sharon's dad died, we went there for the funeral. They buried him next to the house. I remember thinking that was creepy, but not as creepy as when Sharon went out that night after the service, knelt down beside his freshly dug grave, and began screaming. It was so frightening; the only thing drowning out her voice was the loud *banging beat* of my heart. Everyone jumped as the door flung open, each adult stood helpless and speechless, while we children made our way as far under the covers as possible. Through her tears and frightened voice, she said that a light had surrounded her head several times in a fast, circular motion, and she knew it was her dad trying to communicate with her. We were all "bug-eyed scared!" I could say that if I could have escaped, I would have hit the trail; however, I would have had to pass by the "freshly dug grave," so I decided under the covers was the place to be. I remember pulling up the covers over my entire head; reason was, I didn't want to witness anything. Even if it got me, I still didn't want to see it get me. I didn't sleep all night.

Sharon's brother, Cam, was a "tobacco chewin', spittin', overall wearin', what the world would have considered redneck" for certain. His fancy was (whether there was an audience or not) to pull my brothers' pants down around their ankles and just laugh and laugh and laugh, spit, wipe his mouth with his sleeve, then laugh some more. My brothers were humiliated and I was furious. We hated to see him coming.

Life there was bizarre, to say the least. It was like stepping into a legendary "Hillbilly World," with white lightnin' and fights (I mean real, blood flying, black-eyed bruising fights) between husband and wife. I remember several times walking in after school and seeing hunks of hair on the floor mingled with blood and glass. It was often a fearful place.

We traveled with Dad on occasion and frequently went to meet his love. We stopped at a fairly nice home. In a driveway sat a state trooper's car. Dad would knock on the door, as it opened, a man would take something from Dad, and he would hand Dad something in a brown bag. Dad would return to the car, put the bag in the trunk, get back in the car, then we'd leave, that was, until the next time. I later learned that man, the state trooper, whose duty was to protect so to say, was my dad's source of "white lightning." I've wondered if that man knew what he contributed to, other than his own wallet.

One Christmas I wanted to buy gifts for my brothers, but I

had no way of doing it. Although I did chores and cooked, I didn't get an allowance. I thought just maybe, because I was always good about my duties, I possibly might earn enough to buy gifts. But instead of asking if I could earn, I asked if I could borrow from my dad.

"May I borrow twenty dollars to buy Christmas presents?" He looked at me long and hard and said, "Sure, for a trade!" His words frightened me, and although he had never given me any cause to believe that he was that kind of man, his words, laced with the heavy odor of alcohol, made me believe many negative actions could be possible at that very moment. He didn't have to say anything more; I just backed away. I never asked for another favor. *What is wrong with me?* I wondered.

We moved to Jonesborough, about ten minutes from where we had been living, to a four-room house with no bath, which meant no shower or tub. Just two bedrooms, a living room, and a kitchen. I had to bathe on the back porch with just a sheet hanging as a shield to hide me from the traffic that came off the hill behind our house. The way we had lived before and how we were living now was an unbelievable contrast.

After repeated bouts with strep throat and tonsillitis, a doctor told me I needed to have a tonsillectomy. Following surgery, when I returned home, my stepmother immediately put me on the front porch to iron. It was a hot, muggy day, and I soon felt faint. When I told Sharon how I felt, all she said was, "Get it done, or I'll call your dad."

My throat was so sore I could hardly swallow, I kept recalling what the doctor had said before I left the hospital: "This is the time you can have all the ice cream and popsicles you want." But it didn't happen. We couldn't afford ice cream, Sharon said.

The next morning I woke up in a blood-soaked bed. Everyone was still asleep, so I went into the kitchen to get a drink because I felt I was strangling. There were only two bedrooms; we children had to sleep in two double beds. Tim, the baby and I slept in the same one, while the other three were crammed in around each other. Suddenly, I heard a scream. Sharon entered the kitchen yelling then shoved me against the wall.

"I thought Tim was bleeding to death, but it was you! Get in there and change those sheets. Wash them out in the tub on the back porch!" I remember crying but also apologizing. Somehow, through all the hurt I still managed to have compassion on her in realizing how scared she was to think Tim was bleeding. God was not happy with the way I was treated; however, those experiences made me sensitive to others who would eventually come into my life abused.

We moved and then we moved again, all the while witnessing Sharon's indiscretions, our dad's wild drunken nights, and the terrible treatment of each other and of us. When he finished fighting with Sharon, he turned on Johnny, Vaughn, and me. Beatings became commonplace. For some unknown reason, he never beat our half-brother or stepbrother. I'm certainly glad of that, but I still wonder why.

Sharon routinely threatened us with: "If you don't do this, I will tell your dad this!"

If her children would break or tear up something around the house, she always blamed it on my brothers. Dad would beat Johnny or Vaughn with a belt. The belt was part of his uniform with Trailways Bus Lines. It was thick and wide and left open wounds as well as bruises. I would always sit and cry in another room.

One day I came into the house and saw broken glass, chairs overturned, and things thrown across the room. I thought we had been robbed. Suddenly, the back door was thrown open and Sharon was screaming, "Don't kill me! Don't kill me!" When she saw me standing there, she yelled, "Run! He's going to kill us. Get Tim and run!"

Tim was asleep in his room, I ran to get him. I felt something hard hit the back of my head, which caused me to black out for a moment. In the same motion I was being yanked backwards with my hair. Dad was holding Sharon's hair with one hand, that's when I realized what hit the back of my head. Apparently, when he forcibly grabbed my hair, the gun (which was in the same hand) hit the back of my head. He didn't care; he clenched his teeth yanked my head towards his face, looked at me with the most hideous demonic eyes and said, "Don't you try to run. I will kill her then go straight down the line." He let go of my hair long enough to aim the gun and added, "I'll kill all of you." I followed the gun as he aimed it in the living room, there sat the boys with fear written all over their faces. As I began to sob, he threw me towards the boys, I landed on the floor. Still holding the gun in one hand, he gripped Sharon's hair tighter, shoved her face against the wall, pointed the gun at her temple, smiled, and pulled the trigger. We all screamed and covered our faces. We knew we were next but, miraculously, the safety was on. She managed to push him away as she ran out the back door then jumped into the car. He ran behind her. Before she could put the car in reverse, he grabbed her door and the steering wheel. By then I had Tim on my hip and ran to the back door where the boys were.

Dad was still holding on to the door, talking in a very pleasant voice to her, begging, "Please get out of the car, and let's talk." She seemed to agree, but as she opened the door, she took both feet and shoved the door into him forcibly, knocking him to the ground. She looked up as she put the car in reverse, saw us, and screamed, "Run, kids, run!" She sped out of the yard, gravel and grass flying behind her, somehow she ran over dad's foot.

Still holding the baby on my hip, I started running, dragging the boys with me, all the while believing dad could be right behind us. That incident took me back to age three and a half, running away with my stolen supper. *I ran faster.*

We found a thickly wooded area and hid for what seemed hours. Finally, we got enough nerve to surface, but when we did, we quickly dashed to an unknown neighbor's house. We told them what had happened. They notified the authorities, and shortly the authorities came, but nothing was done. Back into that black hole we went.

One afternoon, I heard Dad and Sharon screaming at each other. I ran into the kitchen. There I saw Sharon struggling with Dad, her hand reaching behind her as she folded her fingers around a cast iron frying pan. She knocked him to the ground. As he yelled profanities and screamed in pain, she drew back again. I remember screaming but nothing else until they pulled me from a small space between the stove and refrigerator. They began shoving pills down my throat; I gagged and threw them up. Dad began apologizing promising not to let it happen again.

Dad told me he had found evidence of the visitors Sharon entertained while he was gone; his discovery was what caused the first gun incident as well as this one. Her visitors did not come to that house as long as we lived there after those incidents, which, of course, wasn't long.

One day Sharon took us to see Dad at work. From the car, I looked over to my left. I blinked my eyes and then looked again as we approached the woman on the sidewalk. I recognized her from my past, and then I gasped, "That's my mother!"

"Your mother?" Sharon asked, almost laughing. "What do you mean?"

"That's Ruby. I know it is," I insisted.

Sharon responded, "But your mother was a blonde, this woman has black hair. You haven't seen her in nearly ten years."

"I know, but it's her," I firmly stated.

"We'll see. Your dad's right around the corner."

She parked the car, and ran in to where Dad worked. Sharon pulled Dad out to show him the approaching woman, and, to her dismay, he said, "Yep, that's her all right!"

To everyone's dismay, she walked right up to Dad and said, "Heard you have my children."

He answered, "Yes, I do."

She continued, "I'm here to take them back."

"No," he said. "You took them once, gave them away, and you won't get that chance again."

"They were kidnapped from me, I'll see you in court," she flung the words at him as she walked away.

When we finally were told about it, Sharon and Dad were going to court. Ruby was suing for custody. We sat all day long at home, waiting to hear what the court decided. Honestly, I hoped we could go with Ruby, just to get us out of the nightmare in which we were living. *Life*, I thought, *couldn't be any worse*. But her request was denied.

After court, Dad and Sharon started taking us to church at a nearby country church, small in size, and few in attendance. One Sunday morning, as I sat about midway down the aisle, trying to understand what the preacher was saying, a woman behind me suddenly screamed. I shook the rest of the service. I was told later that "the Holy Ghost got a' hold of her." I still didn't quite understand. But thereafter, I tried to make sure that woman was in front of me instead of behind me, just in case that Holy Ghost got a hold of her again. Near the end of that service, some of the church members came around to me and asked if I was saved. I had no idea what they meant, so I asked, "What do you mean?" They told me I was going to hell if I didn't get saved. They asked if I wanted to get saved and, of course, I responded in the affirmative. I had heard of hell, and although I thought we lived there already, I'd do whatever I had to do to keep from going there eternally. They grabbed my arm and literally dragged me to the altar. I don't think I have ever cried that hard before, which the members interpreted as my redemption. I was told I was "saved," and I was also told what I should and should not do to stay "saved." I wanted to be obedient. Sharon and Dad were also persuaded to go to the altar that night. Things were different at home for a time.

We moved again. Then Dad changed jobs and went to work for Eastman Chemical Company in Kingsport on swing shift. Sharon took full advantage of his absence. When he worked night shift, she would go to concerts and invariably bring band members home. She would send us to the basement; I was instructed that we were not to come up until she let us know. Before she'd leave for the concert, she would tell me, "I want this and this done by the time I get home, and if it isn't done, I'll tell your dad I caught you in the alley with a boy." And I knew she would. There wasn't anything she wouldn't do except something good.

Often, she would keep me out of school to do the housework so it would appear that she had been home all day. Once, I didn't get it all done before she came in. I had supper on, did laundry, dusted, and mopped all the floors except the kitchen floor. She did exactly what she said she'd do. She told Dad I was in the alley with a boy, and because I was late getting home, she went looking for me. She told him that I hadn't even been to school all day and for him to check. He did and, of course, I hadn't. I was beaten. We were never spanked. It was always cruel, cruel beatings. I had to listen to how he wasn't going to bring up any "bastards." I was beaten with the same belt he used on my brothers. The beatings were so cruel that there weren't many places on my body not covered with bruises. I had to choose clothes for school that covered those bruises.

The event that was finally the end of our "family" (if that's what you could call it) happened about a week later. Johnny had taken a bath, as he raised himself out of the tub, he grabbed onto the soap dish, pulling it away from the wall. Sharon passed by the door about that time. She witnessed what happened and summoned Dad. He entered the bathroom, removing his belt. I gasped as he began swinging at Johnny, belting him on his wet skin. I can still hear the belt hitting him and Johnny's screams of pain. I covered my ears and cried in agony. Suddenly, as though I had just drunk a cup of courage, something came over me. As he led my brother into the bedroom and closed the door, I became enraged. I could hear him striking Johnny. The walls shook as Johnny fell from one side of the wall to the other. I couldn't stand it anymore. Fear changed to anger, and the protector in me took action. I began beating on the door and screaming for him to stop hurting my brother. The door swung open, there I saw Johnny lying in a fetal position, blood running down his leg.

Dad said, "What do you want?"

I yelled, "I want you to stop beating him! Beat me instead!"

He laughed sarcastically and stated, "Oh, so you want to take your brother's place, do you?" "

Yes," I responded.

"Then take off your clothes and let's get started," he said.

"No! If my clothes come off, you'll have to tear them off!" I screamed back.

He threw the belt over his shoulder and aimed it at me. The belt wrapped around my arm, he then jerked it with such force that I heard a loud noise from inside my shoulder, leaving me in excruciating pain. He continued to strike me, but the pain in my shoulder was so severe that I didn't feel anything else. Later, I realized how severe the beating was. I was covered with bruises all over, and a muscle in my shoulder was torn. I still have problems with my shoulder, but it serves as a reminder of the day I tried to save my brother. It was worth it!

Every morning, my job was to get up and get all the boys ready for school, pack their lunches, and get them out the door quietly without waking Sharon or Tim. But the morning after the terrible beatings, I had a plan. We were going to escape! Instead of packing lunches, I packed a book bag with biscuits and peanut better and jelly sandwiches. In another book bag, I packed a change of clothes for my brothers and me. Then I quietly woke them. Johnny immediately got ready, but Vaughn was too afraid. He kept saying that if we got caught, we'd be beaten. His memory of the events from the night before were still vivid. So we agreed to go without him. We were on a mission, that mission was to get help. My plan would take us to Aunt Corene's house. I would tell her how badly we were treated; she would take us in and then come for Vaughn.

We started our trip to Aunt Corene's house, all the way from Johnson City, Tennessee, to Norfolk, Virginia. Aunt Corene was actually not a blood relative, just a neighbor who had been good to us; we chose a name that showed our affection.

Little did we know how far Norfolk was, nor did we realize the local six o'clock news had us as a feature and was reporting us missing. Law enforcement officers were looking for us. Eventually, we were caught, but not before we had a "Tom Sawyer" adventure. We knew to hide because Dad would probably look for us. We walked all day, and when night fell we slept next to a creek under a bridge. We both changed clothes the next morning. I remember braiding my hair and securing the pigtails with twigs. We thought we would look different if we changed clothes and I changed my hairstyle. Of course, we were wrong. We had decided if anyone stopped us, we would change our names. Johnny would use his middle name. I chose to use one of my names from the past. I decided to use Darlene. I really didn't want to lie, that was the closest to the truth I knew.

The next day we were stopped by a Tennessee State Trooper

about twenty miles from where we started. "What are your names and where are you going?" he asked.

Immediately, I responded with our made-up names and pointed at a brick house about one hundred yards ahead.

He said, "Go on up to your house and go in. I'll make sure you're okay."

We knew we were caught, but we hoped we were wrong. We walked to the house, and as we got to the front we did a quick detour around the back and through the woods. We managed to get away. Just before dark, however, we were stopped again. This time the trooper said, "I know who you are. Why are you doing this?"

I started to cry and beg him not to take us back to our dad's house. I asked Johnny to show the trooper his wounds; he yanked the top of his pants down around his hip. The trooper, certainly taken aback, asked, "How did that happen?"

"My dad..." Johnny started then stopped for a moment to compose himself. "He got mad and whipped me with his belt and his belt buckle."

"Son," started the officer, "that was no whippin'. That was a beatin'!" He then turned to me and asked, "Did you get beaten too? Is that why you're holding your arm that way?"

"Yes, sir, I think he broke something when he hit me with the belt," I replied.

The officer immediately radioed headquarters and said, "These kids are not going back to their father if I have to take them home myself. Is there another place for them? They've been beaten."

Apparently, there was no room in the inn! So we stayed in jail. I have to admit that it was scary, but not as scary as home. We had to tell the policeman what had happened to us. The next day we were placed in a temporary children's home.

I thank God for that state trooper. My dad had to face charges of abuse. In court he stated I got the bruises from playing touch football with a bunch of boys. That really hurt my feelings. I never heard what he said caused Johnny's injuries.

# CHAPTER FIVE

Oakland Park Children's Home was a safe and a very comfortable place to be. The Woodards were wonderful people and cared very much for children. We were the only children there for a while. We worried about Vaughn, but the State said they were checking on him often and that so far he seemed to be okay. He told the State that our dad had been good to him. We knew he was saying what he knew he had better say.

Another family of children arrived and we were excited. Johnny finally had someone to play with besides me. I found a new baby to take care of. Although she was four, that was still enough. I fixed her hair, took her for walks around the park, and played with her. I had a "baby," someone to take care of and someone who became dependent on me. I slept every night with my new little friend. I would bathe her, brush her hair, make sure she brushed her teeth, and dressed her for bed. I would snuggle up to her and tell her a story, and then we'd both drift off to sleep. I loved it! It was the happiest I had been in years. But I still missed Vaughn.

Oakland Park had another visitor, a former resident. He had actually been to Vietnam and lost an eye. I thought it was so intriguing to know someone with a glass eye. I would watch him as he talked to see if I could tell if his eye was fake. I could! *Wow!* That was something! I guess the attention I gave his glass eye made him believe that I had an interest in him.

One night as I slept, I felt someone picking me up. More asleep than awake and too groggy to be sure it wasn't a dream, I didn't protest. At Oakland Park I'd had no fears. I felt myself being laid into another bed; at that point I jumped up, fists drawn. The "Vietnam Visitor," as I called him, whispered, "Let me take you away from all this!" as he grabbed my wrist to pull me closer to him.

"No! I don't want to go anywhere else, I want to be here," I responded in a voice that was loud enough to make my point but not loud enough to wake anyone. As I was trying desperately to pry his fingers off my wrist, I suddenly noticed that this person was not wearing much more than his "birthday suit." That's when I really got mad. "What are you trying to do to me?" I questioned angrily.

He responded, "Shh! You'll get me into trouble, and they'll throw me out of here."

I exclaimed, "So! You should get thrown out of here!"

"I just want to take you away from this sadness, give you a better life," he pleaded.

"I don't want to go anywhere," I protested. "I'm happy here. Don't ever touch me again." I turned to open the door.

"Okay, okay," he pleaded. "Just don't tell."

The next morning, the visitor was gone, leaving a note thanking the Woodards. I never saw or heard from him again, nor did I ever mention anything about that night, until now.

I began believing that I had a certain scent that attracted perverts and predators like flowers attract bees. What was wrong with me?

One warm day, as I sat near the road pitching a ball to my little friend, I was aware that a car stopped near us. A man in the car asked, "Do you know where 8th Avenue is?"

I said, "Yes, it's back that way."

Then he asked, "Where?"

As I stood to point in the direction, I saw that he was totally exposed. I reached down and grabbed my little friend and ran into the house. I immediately told Mrs. Woodard, and she alerted the authorities with the description of the man and the car I had given her. Of course, I never heard anything. After that, I was afraid to go out. I had been robbed again, this time of the mere sweetness of being outdoors. It took several weeks for me to get brave enough to go back out to play—but when I did, I always had a fear. I was constantly looking over my shoulder.

I started to middle school that year. There were boys my age who showed an interest in me. One in particular was Stephen. He was a drummer in a band. The first time I saw him, he was on stage playing in a talent competition at school. I remember the song they played—"Midnight Confession." The girl sitting next to me nudged me and said, "He's looking at you!"

"Who's looking at me?" I asked.

"The drummer," she said in a giddy voice.

"Really?" I asked.

I looked at him, he was watching me! Whoa! I was honestly excited; it was innocent, a very normal situation. He smiled at me, with a heart leaping uncontrollably, I smiled back. Suddenly, *I* felt normal. After the talent show was over (his band won first place), he found me in the hall as I was going back to class. He said, "I've been watching you for days, and I'd like to know your name."

"My name is Rita," I said shyly.

"Well, my name is Stephen. Can I walk you home after school?"

"Yes," I said as I gasped for air.

Stephen walked me home, and to my surprise he lived about three blocks from the Home. I was embarrassed that I didn't have a real home. I hoped he wouldn't pay too much attention to the sign outside and just think I lived in a real nice, real large house. When we got there, he looked startled, but after the initial shock it didn't seem to matter. He was sweet and considerate. His family owned a chain of grocery stores where he sometimes worked after school. At last, someone nice had come into my life, and I was enjoying the healthy attention.

Several weeks later I noticed a car kept going by the Home. The reason I noticed was because sometimes it would turn around in the Home's driveway, go down the street a block, then turn around and come back. *Another weirdo*, I thought, but this time I had some backbone. I marched right out to the street as he came back. He rolled his window down and threw something out. When he had driven out of sight, I went over and picked it up. It had my name on it! I opened it and read the note; its contents asked if I would let the driver of that car stop and talk to me. It was signed *David*. I stood there; the car came back, more slowly than before. He was driving a powder blue 1964 Fairlane 500. He was a bit cocky as he wanted to show me how fast his car would go. He accelerated hard, leaving tire marks on the road for about two hundred yards. He was cool!

He turned around and inched the car up to me and my little friend. Somehow, I didn't feel threatened this time. He rolled the window down and asked, "Can I get out and talk with you?"

"Okay," I said. "What do you want to talk about?"

"Nothing really, just want to talk to you," he responded, chewing his gum like James Dean.

"About what?" I asked.

"Hey, uh, you got a boyfriend?"

"Well, I have someone that walks me home from school," I said.

"Ha! Walks you! I can drive you!" he responded, rolling the gum around in his mouth. "What do you say?"

"I don't know if I'm allowed to ride with anyone," I said.

"Well, ask!" he said quickly.

"Oh, I don't know, but I'll think about it." I turned and waved goodbye, took the hand of my patient little friend and went inside.

I couldn't wait to tell Mrs. Woodard, and she could see how excited I was. Someone was interested in me as a girlfriend—not just one guy, but two. I felt pretty and special.

I had to make a decision. I couldn't have two boyfriends. It was a hard decision, and I didn't enjoy it very much. But, like a typical girl, I chose the boy with the '64 Fairlane. I still couldn't ride in it—after all, I was only twelve—but I loved to watch it come and go. David was a very nice person. He came from a secure home with loving parents. He had several brothers. David was the first boy I truly liked. He was also the first boy who took me for a walk and tried the ole "I love you, so let me get a little closer to you" trick. Though very frightened with the whole "touchy-touchy experience," I made it clear—"No way! I'm going to be a good girl until I get married." Although that's what I protested and what I truly wanted, in the back of my mind I always believed—*I can't be a good girl anymore. My innocence has been stolen from me.*

I made a couple of friends at school who accepted me. I later wished I had said "no way" to their friendship, but I needed acceptance. One day at school they told me they had a secret place in the woods. Somewhat intrigued, I followed them to their hideaway. We only had a few minutes before the school bell rang after our lunch break. I thought we didn't have time to get into trouble. How wrong I was! There were kids in the woods smoking, kissing, "making out," and my "friends" joined the activity. I thought, *I gotta get out of here.*

Just as I turned to go, Vicki grabbed my hand and said, "Don't go back. Let's stay here and have some fun."

My stomach felt queasy. I usually tried to do what was expected of me—I remembered the "hell" described by the people at the little country church—but I finally had some friends and was afraid of losing them.

The bell rang, and my heart jumped. I knew we were about to get into trouble. Some of the guys suggested going for a ride. The girls grabbed my arm and said, "You're in trouble anyway. They're probably walking the halls and calling our parents as we speak. Let's just go!" So I did.

Hours later, the boys said they had to go to work and dumped us out. I followed the girls. We walked a long time. As we walked up a hill, a car came by with three boys in it. They passed us, then their brake lights came on and they backed up.

"Need a ride?" the driver asked.

"No," I said, but Vicki countered, "Speak for yourself. Yes, we need a ride." With flirting eyes and a captivating smile, she got what she wanted.

I protested, "But where are we going?"

"To Asheville! Just get in!" Vicki answered.

I knew we were in *big* trouble for sure. I had no idea where Asheville was, but I knew it was the wrong direction. The guy in the backseat opened his door, got out, grabbed me by the arm, and said, "She's getting in the back with me."

I wanted to cry and wondered how I could have let them talk

me into this. I remembered another time when I was pulled into the backseat of a car; I didn't want to repeat that experience.

Once in Asheville, we went to the apartment of a friend of Vicki's. He was a hippie of sorts but seemed nice enough. We were all tired and wanted to sleep, but he had one bed. I guessed he had given up his bed to us. Not quite! I was awakened by someone's hands caressing my body. I had *also* been in this situation before; I didn't want to be there again. I was enraged, then fearful. I threw his hand off me and moved to the only chair in the place, where I sat the remainder of the night.

The next days the girls somehow were able to get us an apartment in the same complex. I never quite understood what their plan was or how they paid for it. It seemed as though they weren't going home. Every time I asked, they said, "Never." I was freaking out and wondering how we were going to pay for the apartment. I missed my brothers, the Woodards, and home.

I met the manager of the apartments. She was a young woman with a new baby; she kind of took me under her wing. Of course, I gravitated towards her because of her child.

"Where did you come from?" she asked.

"From Johnson City, Tennessee, I want to go back. The girls said they aren't going back," I responded, nearly crying,

"Where are you girls getting your money?" she asked.

"I don't know, because I don't have any," I stated.

Later, I went back to the apartment and the girls were giggling. "What is so funny?" I asked them "Our Hippie friend is sending our supper with some of his friends, all we have to do show them a good time and they'll pay our rent" said Vickie as she straightened up the room. Those words sent up red flags. Although I had no other place to go, I knew I wasn't going to stay there.

"I'll be back later," I said, and went straight upstairs to the manager's apartment.

"Please let me stay here. I don't want to be in that apartment tonight," I pleaded. She asked me why, and I told her. She said I could stay. I didn't even know her name, but she saved me from a situation that would be worse than a nightmare to me. I have often thought I would love the opportunity to thank her.

About thirty minutes after that conversation took place, I heard sirens from police cars and saw flashing lights. They drove up to the apartments and ran into where the girls had been.

"What is going on?" I asked the manager.

"Nothing for you to worry about," she said. "But to be honest, I called the police because of the situation with your friends. You need to go home. I told the police you were with me, so after they pick the others up, they'll come and get you and take you home."

I smiled and hugged her. Even though I knew there would be some punishment, I didn't care; whatever it was...was okay. It took them about twenty minutes to find the girls. The girls had heard the sirens, ran from their apartment, and hid in a cellar space underneath the complex. They put all of us into police cars and took us directly to jail. The police officers took a statement and showed us around. "Do you want to end up in here, living your life like this?" a policewoman asked.

"No, I don't. Can I just go home?" I pleaded.

"Not so soon," the policewoman said. "You'll spend the night here in jail until someone can come after you." I don't remember either of the girls saying a word.

The next day a policeman picked us up and took us home. I was so happy to be back at the Children's Home. I received a good scolding and was advised that I didn't need to allow others to make my choices, that I was responsible for my own actions. I agreed. I was genuinely sorry for what I had done and apologized and apologized. I told the Woodards that at no time did I ever want to be anywhere but at the Children's Home, where I felt safe. I was so glad to see Johnny. Soon, though, life dealt another curve.

A caseworker from the Department of Human Services came to see me and gave me the option of visiting my birth mother, who expressed an interest in me. Every child wants a mother. I kept asking if my brothers were going also, but no one ever answered except to say, "Let's see how this goes with you and then we'll talk about it." *At least I'll be safe*, I thought.

I was finally reunited with my biological mother. I didn't realize then that the option to be united with my biological mother came as an alternative after the State recognized that we had been adopted. Once the State became enlightened, they were legally bound, as were our adoptive parents, to give us back into our adoptive parents' care. At that time, our caseworker spoke regarding the legalities of adoption to our adoptive parents. Our adoptive mother chose to tag me a misfit, a problem child, and uncontrollable, while agreeing to take the boys back. I didn't think I had given anyone any trouble until the Asheville incident. The truth as to why she didn't want me back lay much deeper than the labels she was placing on me.

Ruby—for some reason, I can't call her "Mom"—came back to Tennessee. Actually, she had come to visit her mother, and during that visit she was somehow convinced to take me into her care. Together we boarded a train back to the town where she lived, called Levittstown, Pennsylvania. I was excited sitting next to my real mother. She was telling me all these things we would do together. She told me about her young son, my little brother Michael. He was eighteen months old. I couldn't wait to see him. His dad was a construction worker. We talked about all the things there was to do for girls my age, including a teen club across the street from their house.

*Wow! This is great,* I thought. *Finally, I belong to someone who wants me.* In my heart I forgave her for giving us up at first. *People make mistakes,* I reasoned. What mattered was that she wanted her daughter back. I hoped that all of us would be together soon.

We arrived in Levittstown and went straight to a job site where her husband was working. I was shocked when I saw him. He was much younger than she, quite handsome, tanned, dark hair, dark eyes, and very masculine. What was she thinking? She was a pretty woman, but even at the age of twelve I could figure that he was at least ten years her junior.

We picked up her son, Michael, from the person who watched him while she was gone. He was so adorable. He had the same coloring as his dad and was friendly and playful. I had such a sweet time with him.

When we arrived at her home, I was pleased to see that it was pretty but modest in size and furnishings. I was eager to see the "hang out" she had told me about. At my age, that was something pretty intriguing. When I parted the curtains, though, I saw a big, undeveloped, wooded hill. I should have recognized the red flags that warned me of trouble, but this was my mother, *she wanted me*. I could ignore a few things.

Shortly after arriving at her house, there was a knock at the door. Ruby yelled for whoever it was to come in, and when the visitor entered the house, Ruby said, "Michelle, let me introduce you to someone." They came around the corner to my room where I was playing with Michael. As she pointed towards me, she said, *"Michelle, this is my niece."* I must have looked as dumbfounded as I felt. "Rita," she paused then said, "this in my neighbor."

Her words rang in my ears. *Niece*, I thought, *I'm not your niece*, but as usual I didn't say anything except "Nice to meet you."

A third red flag had been thrown, but this time I realized that even though I had accepted her, she couldn't accept me. I wanted to go home right then. I did go home shortly after that, knowing I would never return.

Although Michael was our brother, we lost contact with him over the years. However, he was able to track us down. His feelings about Ruby were much the same as ours. However, she was in and out of his life more frequently because the little towns they lived in were very close to each other.

He shared with us that he'd had a terrible time knowing the truth of his identity. He believed for years he was a McDonald, when suddenly, his stepfather, Rocky (who is one of the finest people we had ever met), found a birth certificate bearing his first name and birth date with a strange last name, "Peck." Suddenly, we realized that after my dad, Ruby had married a man by the name of Peck, had four children by him, and left them all to be raised by grandparents. The reasons are too unbelievable to record (definitely another book), but what we will say is that she apparently was still married to Peck when she became expectant with Michael, whose real father was McDonald. Michael has two last names, while I, at age of four, had no first name. Ha! What's really strange is that both men were purportedly murdered, by her own account in a personal, deep, supposedly honest moment while explaining to me why she did not raise her other four children.

All I really found out about the other children were their names, Debbie, Connie (or Donna), Philip, and James.

What I did not know then was that returning to my mother had been my adoptive mother's idea and the State's hope of a perfect match. My adoptive mother did not want me back. I was totally unaware of this plan, but it backfired on all of us.

One of the things I learned during all of this was that when you adopt a child, it is a binding legal contract. You cannot "un-adopt" a child. You can give away your own flesh and blood, but when you sign an adoption contract, it stands forever. It makes me think of the relationship God has with us, which is unlike human love where often commitments are fleeting. The Bible tells us in Ephesians that we are God's adopted children. It stands forever, and He will never give us up.

At a closed-door hearing, I was asked if I wanted to live with Ruby. My answer was a definite *no*. But little did I know about the events that were about to transpire. She may have been the lesser of two evils. I went back to live at Oakland Park, where at least I was with my brother again.

Upon returning from school one day, Mrs. Woodard met Johnny and me at the door. "You'll never guess what has happened," she told us. "Your adoptive parents have been contacted and they want you all back."

Every breath in my body evaporated and I began to hyperventilate, which was not exactly the response she expected. But how could I expect her to understand? I had never told anyone my experiences in their home. "I can't go back. Please don't send me back," I pleaded.

Mrs. Woodard knew me and knew what she was seeing was genuine fear. She contacted my social worker, Mrs. Thomas, who, I learned much later, had become a friend and correspondent of my adoptive mother. Mrs. Thomas asked me question after question. I was painfully truthful. She responded to my answers in a way that made it evident to me that she didn't believe me.

"I believe you have a boyfriend you do not want to leave," she accused.

"Yes, I do have a boyfriend, but that's not the reason I don't want to go back. My adoptive dad has hurt me, he won't leave me alone. Please!" I begged.

My pleas fell on deaf ears. Our tickets were bought to return us to our adoptive parents, who were living in Turkey.

I had to tell David goodbye, but I also shared with him my fears, something I would have never done, which showed the point of my despair. He heard my cries and realized how serious this was and that the State wasn't listening. He conceived a plan. Plans always got me in trouble!

Just a few weeks before we were supposed to leave for Turkey, I packed a brown paper bag full of clothes and walked out of those walls of security one warm, dark night. David drove me away. We had no idea where we were going—just someplace where we could get married so he could save me from the dreaded torment of where I was headed. I had just had my thirteenth birthday.

We ended up in South Carolina, where we heard you could get married without your parent's signature. Before long we were pulled over by a State Trooper. David had surreptitiously changed his license plates from Tennessee to Arkansas plates, which had belonged to one of his uncles. The State Trooper didn't believe our story because he already knew the truth. Returning to Tennessee, the only question I can recall being asked of either of us was if any intimate activity had occurred between us. We both answered no, which was the truth.

# CHAPTER SIX

In late summer of 1967, my brothers and I were on a plane bound for Turkey. I had no doubts that plane was heading me on a collision course. I could feel it coming. I could do nothing more than I had done. I had yelled, begged, and even run away, but no one seemed to care enough. I was a victim waiting to be victimized again and I knew it.

Our parents met us at the airport in Ankara. It seemed a much nicer reunion than I had anticipated. Mother seemed genuinely happy to see me. It made the transition easier. She and I stayed up half the night talking. She told me, "You now are the daughter I always wanted." That made me happy.

The next morning she went to the beauty shop before I awoke. The sudden touch of a hand on my body immediately awakened me. There he sat on my bed. I summoned the courage and, through clenched teeth, I said, "Don't you ever lay your hands on me again. Don't you ever touch me again."

He chuckled and said, "Well, I know you're still a good girl, 'cause if you wouldn't let me, you wouldn't let anyone." Again I smelled the odor of alcohol. I knew for certain I was back in hell.

We lived in the town of Trabzon, located on the Black Sea. I had to go to school some five hundred miles away in Ankara, which meant boarding school. I loved it, and I never got into any trouble. Nightly happenings in the dorms became the next day's conversations. The worst thing I did was hide in the closet from my roommate and then laughed so hard I wet my pants just thinking about how she would look when she opened the closet. When she came back to the room though, I was on the floor cleaning up.

I always dreaded going home, except that I would get to see my brothers. Trabzon was a small fishing town nestled between hills and the Black Sea. Merchants were set up along sides of the roads to sell their products. The house we lived in was on the Black Sea, and it didn't take long to understand where it got its name: the sand is black. The most amazing thing about our house was an actual Turkish toilet, nicely crafted, though it was a mere hole in the floor. A place was embedded in the floor to position your feet as you stood over the hole. After living there for a while, you couldn't help developing great thigh muscles.

When I went home for Thanksgiving holidays, Mother (I called her "Mother" although I no longer felt that relationship with her) was in bed with the flu. I tried to help her by being at her beck and call. But life in that home hadn't changed. Because there were only two bedrooms in the house, I made my bed on the couch in the living room, facing the Sea. I loved to see her white-capped waves and hear them crashing on the shore at night. However, the sweet sounds were shattered the night I heard the sound I had learned to dread: my adoptive dad's voice. He was there again, and before I could do anything, he picked me up and was carrying me. I fought, shoved on his face, chest, and arms. He was six foot three inches tall and weighed between two hundred and fifty to two hundred and seventy five pounds. I was almost five foot four inches and weighed maybe a hundred and ten pounds. During the struggle, Mother must have been awakened, because I heard her yell, "Let her go! Leave her alone!" He said he felt sorry for me sleeping on the couch and was bringing me into their room so I would rest there. After that, I climbed into bed with her and felt safe because she had saved me. She told him to sleep on the couch. That was the last time I ever saw her in a protective mother role.

I was happy when it was time for me to return to school in Ankara in the fall of 1967. Flying back to Ankara, we heard the news of war between Turkey and Cyprus. I don't remember being afraid. I was actually in the air when the war started. The lights on the plane were turned off, and we landed with just the instrument panel. Lights at the airport were also shut down. We were met at the airport with cars that had black felt over the lights. It was an amazing time for this young girl. Those of us who were returning to school could not go back until the war ended because our school was on the military base. I should have been afraid, but after what I had been through, this was a piece of cake.

American children at that school had a "sponsor family." If our parents were not close by, that family supplied our emergency needs. My sponsor parents picked me up at the airport and took me to their home. Their home was very nice in an apartment complex called The Star Apartments. Each arm of the star was an individual grouping of high-rise apartments. In the center was a huge opening to the outdoors. When it rained, it rained down in the middle of that complex. I loved that place.

During the wartime, I stayed with them. We were not allowed to have lights on at night—only candles. It was not as easy for the enemy planes flying over to detect where we were. However, one night I was awakened by loud gunshots. Everyone in the apartment jumped up, thinking we had been attacked. Later we learned that a couple hosting a party had been told to turn off their lights, when they ignored the order, the Turkish Military Police returned to the couple's apartment and shot them dead because "they put everyone else in danger." After everything settled down, I returned to school, very happy to be back in safe surroundings.

Going home for Christmas was even worse. My parents decided to attend a military Christmas party on base, and decided to take me. I wasn't old enough at thirteen, but going to a party was exciting. It was one of the most horrific nights of my life. That night is burned into my memory alongside the tub incident with Johnny. It started in a lounge area. There was a band playing. My dad immediately went over to the bar and sat down. Mother and I went to a table. No sooner had we sat down than a young enlisted man came and asked me to dance. Mother nudged me to go on, then a man asked her to dance. One song blended into another, so there was no pause to sit down. Everyone kept dancing. The music was very loud. Suddenly, people began running off the dance floor, things started flying, glasses were breaking, chairs were thrown, and the music stopped. A group of men were trying to hold someone back, then I saw Mother holding her head and people attending to her. I screamed and ran to help her then noticed the man being restrained was my dad. He was being held by several men as he was yelling and screaming. The military police appeared, but Dad started after Mother. The MPs finally put a straightjacket on him and administered a sedative, but that didn't work soon enough and a second dose was given.

What I hadn't seen, but was later told, was that he had gotten up from the bar, went over to Mother and pulled her by the arm from her dancing partner. He began punching and throwing her around, yelling, "I brought two women with me and neither wants to dance with me." I was so scared and embarrassed that I wanted to die.

Someone offered to take Mother and me home, but instead we went to the home of an officer and his Turkish wife, where my brothers had stayed while we went to the dance. Mother was badly bruised and cut. She was only four foot eleven and certainly could not fight off a man as big and as inebriated as he was. It was a horrible sight. The next day the military police brought our dad to the officer's home where we were. He immediately fell to his knees and asked Mother for forgiveness. He said that it was the alcohol and not him that acted that way. She accepted his apology. (A few months later that officer died of a massive heart attack, and several years later, after Mother and Dad were divorced, the Turkish widow married Dad.)

We went back to our house. Dad took a walk on the beach. Mother found the gun Dad kept in the house and hid it somewhere else. She saw me watching and said, "He's very ashamed of himself. I'm afraid he would try to do something to end his life."

When he came in from his walk, he went straight back to their bedroom. Mother followed and closed the door. I heard her say, "It isn't there anymore." I never knew what his intentions were, but she must have been as afraid of him at that moment as I was.

One day while in my dorm room, I received a message that I had a visitor. I was delighted to receive a visitor, but my delight quickly became shock when I saw my Dad. He immediately said, "I've got some good news!"

"Really? What is it?" I asked.

He responded with the broadest smile I'd ever seen on his

face. "I'm being transferred here. You won't have to live away from home anymore."

Why, when my life brought me happiness, did it always throw me back to where I had come from? The room started spinning, and I tried to smile in the presence of the office staff, but I could feel I was losing touch with reality.

We moved into a beautiful apartment next door to a Turkish school. The whole side of the school facing my room was glass windows, and I enjoyed watching the activities of a different culture. They prayed often. I could see even the janitors take out a little rug several times a day and kneel at those windows to pray.

I became acquainted with the Hutton family, who lived two floors above us. Mr. Hutton worked for the United Nations. They were from Canada. Their daughter, Lynn, became a friend to me. The school held a pageant, and out of my ninth grade class I was nominated to participate. I couldn't believe my schoolmates thought I was pretty enough to be sponsored by the whole class. I felt special. My parents didn't attend. I guess it wasn't something they wanted to support. The Huttons told me they were going to act as my parents. They made that night very special.

Although I didn't win (a gorgeous senior did), I became known to other students. I was asked to special parties, dances, and gatherings at the homes of kids whose parents lived in Ankara. It was a fun time.

I especially remember a birthday party for a guy whose father was a general in the military. The party was held on the first floor of the complex where they lived. Rumor had it that they resided on three floors of that building. I thought I was mingling with "the upper crust of society." I had my first taste of a screwdriver that night. I was told it was orange juice. One sip and it didn't last long in my mouth. It was nasty! Everyone got a big laugh out of that, but I couldn't forget the things I had been told in that little country church that would send me to hell.

The abuse in our house continued, and everyone knew it, but the pain it caused did not compare to the emotional pain Mother inflicted on me. She called me into the dining room one afternoon and directed me to sit down. She pushed a dish of some kind of dessert toward me.

"What is it?" I asked.

She only said, "Just try it."

I tasted it, but it was nasty. I swallowed the bite I had in my mouth and realized she was grinning. Her next words are indelibly etched in my memory. "Ha! You're not a good Christian anymore. That donut was soaked in alcohol! You say a good Christian doesn't drink, so I guess this means you aren't a good Christian."

I was devastated. I had tried very hard to live my life the way I was told I should since that night at the altar. Now I was doomed and I was going to hell, and my very own mother unlocked the door and pushed me in. I left the table crying. I just didn't understand. Thank God the understanding I had about salvaging salvation was eventually revealed as untrue.

My room was my refuge. Alone most of the time, there was safety, except at night. One evening as I sat doing my homework, Dad came in and said, "You realize you're pretty enough to be in the movies?"

"No," I said, hoping he would hurry and leave.

"Well," he continued, "I have connections. We could get you started, and you could be a star."

I looked at him and asked, "What would I have to do?"

"Well, we would first start by filming your daily routine: getting up, getting ready for school, going to school, coming home, everything all the way to night. Of course, we'd have to follow you into the shower and getting ready for bed."

As he spoke, I rose out of my chair and said, "No! No! Get out of my room and leave me alone."

His response was a tremendous shove that threw me against the wall, and I began to cry.

"I pay for this place. I'll leave when I want to!" he said in a stern whisper.

At that point, the door swung open and there stood Mother. "Get out!" she said.

As he knocked her backwards, he left my room. She just stood there looking at me while I cried, but it wasn't a look of love or concern. It was a look of disgust, and I knew she hated me.

I shared with my friend, Lynn, from upstairs about what was going on. I cried to her uncontrollably. I just needed to talk with someone. I had no one. I felt better. She told me it wasn't right and that my mother was just as wrong as my dad. She told me I could come to her home anytime, no matter what time.

The next day Mother had been shopping and wasn't home when I got there, so I went to my room to do my homework. I heard her come in. She walked back to my room, opened the door, and threw something on my bed. Then she said, "I bought that for you so you won't get raped." Her voice was so filled with sarcasm that it ripped a little more of a heart that was already in shreds. She had bought a chain door lock.

That night, guess who put the door lock on? The funny thing is the chain lock also had a master key that you could slip under it and unlock it from the other side. Guess who had the key? A night or two later I awakened to a noise. Sure enough, it was him opening my new lock. She caught him and took the key. I was so thankful. I could sleep at last. But I still knew she hated me, and I hated that.

I started putting a tin trash can at my door so if he somehow found the key and opened the door, the crash would wake me and, I hoped, her as well.

Several weeks later it happened. He must have hunted until he found the key, but he got a surprise. The loud bang that the trash can made had its intended effect. It woke me *and* Mother. She asked him for the key, and he told her that I had actually let him in and that he didn't have a key. I guess she wanted to believe him, so she called me "a little tramp" and forcefully shut the door.

At this point, it didn't hurt anymore. I was numb, but for some reason my main objective was just to survive. Little did I realize what an impact these situations were making on my psychological well being.

On the night that changed everything, I had been asleep. I had devised a way to twist my ankles around each other to secure my legs closed; I got in the habit of sleeping that way. I remember coming into awareness that night and realizing I could open my eyes, but that's all I could control. I could not move my arms or legs. Suddenly, there appeared a figure of a man positioned somewhat like Rodin's bronze statute of *The Thinker* sitting right about my knees on my bed. It was transparent, but a light outlined his body and flashed three times. Feeling overwhelming fear, the tears fell but, unable to move my arms or hands, I could not wipe them away. At that moment, I was certain I was losing my mind, I cried out to God. I had never called on Him before, but he was all the hope I had. I prayed, *"God, please hear me, please be there. I know I'm going crazy. Please don't let me."*

As soon as I said those words, I heard a voice that only my mind could hear: "Close your eyes, relax, and go to sleep. You will be okay." And that's exactly what I did. The next thing I remember is waking up and feeling a peace that everything was all right. I could move again.

The next evening, as I did my homework, Dad came into my room. He asked me how I was doing, and I told him fine. Then he bent over and whispered, "How about leaving your door unlocked for me tonight?" The whiskey smell was so strong it made me sick.

I responded, "No!"

He sneered and said, "I'll get in if I want in," and threw my door back against the wall as he staggered from the room.

The following afternoon, after spending that night and the next day in torment, I made some inquiries about a psychiatrist and how to get an appointment. A friend knew one personally and made an appointment for me that day. It was a family psychiatrist. After school, I rode a bus to where his office was instead of going home. I immediately felt comfortable with him, and I opened up and told him everything, then asked, "What can I do to be different? Something is wrong with me. Help me to change so these things won't keep happening."

His answer was not what I expected. He said, "It's not you. If you weren't there, it would be whoever was there. Let me call your dad and let's talk about this."

"Oh, no, you can't!" I protested. "He'll be so angry at me. I'll get into so much trouble."

"Well, I want to help you, but I can't continue without your parent's permission for one thing, and the other thing is, who's going to pay the bill?"

I felt like I had been dashed with ice water. I sat speechless for a moment, and then I stood and left his office. I had run into a brick wall again. I never once thought about money. It took money to get help. No money, no help!

I was late getting home. Mother met me at the door and said in a stern voice, "Where have you been?"

"I took the wrong bus," I told her.

"I don't believe you!" she screamed. Then she took a piece of paper in her hand and shoved it in my face. "This is where you've been."

I pulled back her hand to see a note. I recognized it as a letter that had been given to me by my friend, Colleen. Her apartment complex was right across the street from where the school bus picked us up and dropped us off. It had been written by a young man whom I had never seen, but he often saw me through his apartment window in the mornings. I never responded, but I kept the note just because it was kind of nice to read that someone thinks you're pretty. His exact words were, "You look like a flower." It was one of the most innocent things in my life.

I explained to her that I had never met that person, I just kept the note. She again told me I was lying white trash. I took a deep breath, not caring if it was right or wrong. I said, "Okay. I was at the office of a psychiatrist."

She suddenly turned pale and said, "Why?"

I told her I went to see what was wrong with me. I wanted horrible things to stop happening to me.

She asked, "How much did you tell him?" I said, "Everything." She grabbed me by the shoulders and shook me, screaming, "Do you realize what you've done? You've just cost your dad his job. Once that gets out, they will let him go." I broke down. How much worse could things get?

The next day my friend, Lynn, said her parents wanted to

talk with me. I went upstairs and they sat me down. Her dad said Lynn had told them what was going on in my house. I started to cry.

"Don't cry." he said. "We have contacted the State of Tennessee to let them know what is going on in your house. We are presently seeking the knowledge of how to go about bringing you into our family. If you choose to join us, this is what we do as a family. These are our rules, and these are the benefits." I was so excited, but I knew I couldn't act like it when I went home.

For some reason, dad's job took him away. It was nice because that was the first night I could remember sleeping with my bedroom door open since I returned to my adoptive family.

One morning shortly after dad left, I was awakened by something bouncing on my bed. I jumped up to see Mother standing there and a suitcase on my bed. "Pack it," she said.

"Where am I going?" I asked.

"All the way back to the States. We're leaving today, so get up." She was obviously in a hurry.

I got out of the bed and began packing. I was so confused and so excited at the same time. "Are my brothers going?" I asked.

"No, just the troublemaker," she replied. I just dropped my head and continued to pack.

"May I go tell the Huttons goodbye?"

"No!" she said.

As soon as I showered and readied myself, she said, "Let's go." Out the door we went, and I didn't look back. I wanted to say goodbye to my brothers but she wouldn't let me. My heart was already missing them.

Mother and I arrived in the United States and, although I was happy to be out of that house and away from everything that had happened to me there, my heart yearned for Johnny and Vaughn. We had never been that far away from each other, and I felt that I had left a big part of my life behind.

We spent the next month in Norfolk, Virginia, at the home of a Mr. and Mrs. Rogers. They were extremely nice to me and made me feel at home. I knew we weren't going to stay there, but I wondered when things were going to change again. I knew another phase of my life was about to take place, but through all these events I had learned to take not one day, but one moment at a time.

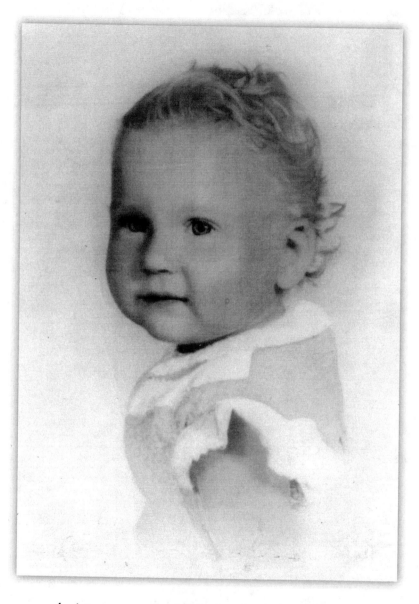

A picture my paternal Grandmother had. Once I was
reunited with my dad, she gave me a copy. She said I
was about one year old.

"Wake Up Sleepy Head"
Me, about eighteen months old, my dad and Johnny,
about six months old.

Age five or six
Me and my guitar.
Before the "pixie" haircuts.

Me and my sweet brothers
in Italy. Ages four, three and two.

My brothers and I with some friends in Italy.
Ages five, four and three.

Our special "Aunt Coreen" just before we left Virginia,
bound for our biological dad's home.

Me at age sixteen.

My "intervention" family, Mom and Dad Hutchins, myself
at age fifteen, Camille, Ralph and John.

Homecoming - Greeneville High School - 1970
Courtesy of the The Greeneville Sun

Jim, my Dad Hutchins and me.

My daughter Heather to the far left and my friends.

Me speaking at the Annual Holston Methodist Conference at Lake Junaluska in North Carolina.
Look who came to help me.

Our biggest blessings, besides our children.

My Mom and Dad Hutchins

# CHAPTER SEVEN

About six weeks after arriving back in the States, I was told it was time to pack again. I don't remember how we got to Tennessee. We arrived at a place called Holston United Methodist Home for Children in a small town called Greeneville. It was a very small children's home, but very pretty and sweet, nestled in the mountains of East Tennessee. Greeneville was the most beautiful place I had ever been—so clean, neat, and it seemed to offer a haven. Mrs. S (as I had come to address her after she forbade me to call her "Mother") told me the administrator said I could live there because of the issues at home. This move was merely to protect me, she said. Whatever the reason, it was okay because I was far, far away from torment. I was happy, with the exception of missing my brothers.

Life in my new surroundings started off pretty well. There were six cottages, each built to accommodate ten children. There were four for girls and two for boys. I shared a room with Kathy, who was a pretty girl my age, but very angry, and she knew how to elicit pity to get her way. I recall her slamming our door and screaming at the house parents while they stood on the other side of the door. She would say things like, "You don't know what it's like to be a child without parents. You don't know what it's like when all your friends have a home to go to and you don't." All the while she'd be grinning at me. I learned a lot of tactics there, although I can honestly say I never used them.

As time went on, it became more and more difficult to get along with so many children, most of them from homes as dysfunctional as mine. Each had their own set of problems and demons. Some of these children had actually witnessed the murder of their parent, sometimes by the other parent. Some were just dropped off; some were wards of the State. Some would attack others personally, either verbally or physically. I was never attacked, but my clothes were. I found them in shreds in the top of my closet.

Even with all that, those were minor things compared to what I had experienced. I could sleep at night without any worries. From time to time, I still experienced nightmares about the night of my paralyzing fear. I would always remember that first time and what I was told to do, and even though these later times were dreams, I took that knowledge into my dream world and utilized it as though I were awake. It always worked. Divine intervention, even in my dreams.

I arrived at the children's home in the late spring of 1968. Spring soon turned to summer. We all had assigned chores. We worked hard in vegetable gardens, cleaning house, and cleaning the administrative offices on Saturdays. I didn't mind. I was part of a team, kind of a family, and eventually some of us would be as close as family.

It was nearing the first day of school, and the girls in the cottage got together and started talking. One looked at me and said, "Just so you won't be surprised, you won't be accepted very well."

"Why not?" I asked.

"Because you're too different," she replied, and the other girls agreed. That certainly gave me something to think about as I anticipated that first day in a new high school.

The first day of school turned out to be a good experience. People were very friendly. I had assumed the girls from the home were right, but they were so wrong. Some at school had heard before I actually started school that someone was coming from a foreign country. The boys thought I was from Sweden, evidently because of my blonde hair and blue eyes. I heard another rumor that my dad was the new chief officer at the local Magnavox factory. That rumor soon got dashed when I got on and off the Holston Home bus every day.

Before long I had friends, both wealthy and those not-so-wealthy. I was nominated secretary-treasurer of the sophomore class, which made me a part of the Student Council. I only held that office for that year because, living at the Children's Home, I had no transportation to and from meetings, and we weren't allowed to ride with anyone. But life was so good. Actually, life was great!

I got a part-time job in a beauty shop, sweeping up hair, washing out brushes, dusting, filling up shampoo bottles. It made me feel independent. My life was finally going great. I still missed my brothers, and sometimes at night I would cry for them. I made a total of five dollars a week working two afternoons after school and some on Saturday's.

Johnny and Vaughn finally called me at Christmas. They had returned to the States and were living in Norfolk, Virginia. Our parents had divorced. The boys told me Dad wouldn't let her live with him after she returned from the States. They said he told her he wanted a divorce because she took me away. It was ironic—she took me away to save her marriage and it still ended, but she never came back to get me. I thank God for Holston Home. They accepted me and saved me from all the cruel things when no one else seemed to care. I now see that it was divine intervention. God knew me and had plans for me even when I didn't know Him.

During my sophomore year, I met a boy who was cute, sweet, funny, and he played football. His name was Billy. I met him through my friend Catherine. Catherine was a beautiful, fun-loving, people-loving, rich girl. She was the youngest girl of five children. Her happiness came from being good to people. She was funny, and I loved being near her because she helped me to feel normal. I remember that Catherine and her mother's favorite show, which they often watched together, was "I Love Lucy." Catherine would impersonate Lucy, Desi, and Steve Martin... She kept me in stitches! Her home life seemed happy, but I always wondered. She made everyone around her feel special. Any time she would go on a trip, she would always bring me back something special. I loved Catherine. At one point, Mr. Bird, her dad, tried to see about adopting me, but the Children's Home said I was already adopted and could not be adopted twice. I was upset then because I felt it was unkind; a family wanted me, but now I know the Home did the right thing. However, I loved and still love that family.

My other "best friend" was Trudy. The first time I saw her she was wearing the smallest bikini swimsuit I had ever seen. She was shaking out a sheet, getting ready to lie in the sun. A van from the Children's Home took a group of children, including me, to the local swimming pool. The van nearly leaned over on two wheels as all the boys moved on the side where she was. She was petite and beautiful. She became one of my dearest friends. I'd always admired her. She was smart and secure. She radiated a sense of security that I lacked. In hindsight, I realize this was one of the reasons I loved being around her, besides the fact she was pretty and got a lot of attention, which, of course, blew onto whomever was with her. Nobody messed with her! I learned from her that you can take a stand for yourself and still be likeable, and that being pretty doesn't mean you're dumb. She hasn't changed in all these years, petite and secure, she has all the world could offer, and she is still my friend.

I made very special friends, but some just stood out more than others. One of those was Edith. Her parents owned the local newspaper. I can never say enough about how her family touched my life. Whenever they saw me, they would always embrace me. They have had no idea how special they made me feel. They opened their home, gave me a shower when I got married. They always acknowledged the births of my children. Edith's Governess, "Dumplin'," always sent me cards on my children's birthdays. In a Father's Day issue of *The Greeneville Sun*, Edith's mother, who had a column called "Cheerful Chatter," wrote about my children, recognizing what wonderfully beautiful children they were and how proud their father must have been. How special that was for me. They helped shape my healthy life. I will forever be indebted to them.

Edith spent some very special time with me. I think she tried to be the mother that was absent in my life—and I appreciated it. She talked to me about boys and shared information with me that either her mother or her governess had shared with her. The first car wreck I was ever in was with her. It's funny now, but then we all thought we were dead. We should not have skipped the last class of school that day. I was never truant again.

Billy was great fun. He laughed a lot and made me laugh.

Everybody loved Billy. Even though we had been a couple for quite some time, I was not allowed to date until the end of my sophomore year. On our first real date, he found a place where we were alone. He began getting fresh, and I began to cry. I cried so much that he started crying. Before that night was over, we both were laughing about us crying. At Christmas, Billy gave me a pre-engagement ring. I had never felt so important to anyone in my life. I was so excited. By the end of my junior year, I definitely knew I cared about him, but not enough to live with him forever. Breaking up with him was my saddest time since I had moved to Greeneville. I knew *I* was going to hurt someone.

During the summer following my sophomore year, I occasionally had an opportunity to babysit for the Hutchins family. Charles Hutchins was the assistant executive director at Holston Home, and he and his wife had three children. Toward the end of the summer, Mr. Hutchins summoned me to his office and told me that their daughter, Camille, wanted me to be her sister. The Hutchins wanted to take me into foster care. I felt so privileged. I readily agreed and moved into their home as soon as the offer was made. Their house was on the campus of the Children's Home. It was so close, yet it felt so far away.

Before I go on sharing information concerning my new family, I must tell you that through counseling, I met a particular counselor who ultimately gave me a fierce desire to attain what she told me was unattainable. She told me that I lived in a fantasy world. She offered that conclusion after I told her my desire for the future was to get married to someone who would adore me and I would adore him. We would have a large family and live happily the rest of my life our lives. Her reaction did not paint a pleasant future for me. She said what I wanted was non-existent. Soon I would find she was wrong.

My new family had all the qualities of the near-perfect family. As I mentioned, Mr. Hutchins was assistant administrator of the very children's home where I was a resident. It was evident the love he had for all children. He was a praying man, kind, considerate, well-respected, and forever in ministry to children and God. He was the best example I had ever had of a near-perfect father, and he adored his wife and their children.

Mrs. Hutchins was a homemaker. She was loving, kind, soft-spoken and very balanced—the best example of what a mother should be. She, too, was a Christian and was very active in church, where she directed the choir and was an officer in United Methodist Women.

I had always had an innate love of children and a need to take care of them. The Hutchins' children were no exception. Camille, then eight years old, was eager to share her room with me. She made room in the closet and the chest of drawers for my clothes and seemed to easily take me into her physical and emotional space.

Ralph and John were a bit more of a challenge. Their two heads were together a lot, and I didn't always understand their language. There were very close in age—then four and three years old. The Hutchins adopted Ralph when he was about five months old, and less than a week after they brought him home, Mrs. Hutchins realized she was pregnant again. Everyone adored Ralph. He was very mischievous but always kept us laughing. John was a little more subdued. He was the cute little teddy bear who always climbed into his mother's lap, his arms wrapped around her neck. He couldn't have cared less about anything else while he was there. I remember him crying for his mother the first time or two I babysat. I would pick him up, hold him the way she did, and rock him in her rocking chair. He would cuddle up and stop crying. That was special.

One event I must share was the day the brothers destroyed the "Little Green Army Men." I recall sitting at the kitchen table one Saturday morning. I believe I was going over some homework. Both the boys were still in their little footed pajamas, playing with their little green plastic soldiers. They both came in the kitchen and shoved a chair over to the counter. I stopped what I was doing to see what they were about to do. They looked at each other, and I somehow knew something major was about to happen. Before I could stop them, they both dropped their plastic Army men into the toaster and pushed the control down. I later realized that they probably expected the little soldiers to pop back out like they had seen bread so many times. I yelled for Mrs. Hutchins, and she came running. The toaster was smoking and smelled terrible, and the little green Army men were toast. The actions taken by Mrs. Hutchins that day were actions and reactions that changed my life. As I watched her concern for her two little boys and the conversations that followed, I questioned her handling of it. As she picked up the smoking toaster and set it outside, I asked, "Is that all you're going to do?"

"What did you expect me to do?" she asked.

"Well, they ruined your toaster. Shouldn't they get spanked?"

She paused, smiled, looked at me, and said, "That's just a toaster. It's a thing. I can get another one. The boys certainly didn't intend to melt their toys, nor did they intend to ruin the toaster. At least they didn't get hurt."

Oh, my goodness! People are more important than things! My experience had always been that children, especially, were less important than things. Where I had lived, there was no room for accidents. That word was only used when it had to do with cars. On that day everything I had previously learned or experienced went up in the smoke rolling from the toaster. That was just one of the many lessons I learned in the short twenty-two months in their home.

What a blessing this new family was to me. Some of the many things I learned while living with the Hutchins family were unconditional love, patience, kindness—and that was special. Not one time did I ever feel like a foster child. What was done for one was done for the others. They protected me, and when I broke rules I was gently disciplined. I was allowed to go out with Billy on Saturday night but was told to be in by ten o'clock. The first time I had a date, I was fifteen minutes late getting home. They didn't say anything to me. I thought they had let it slide.

The next time I had a date, Mr. Hutchins casually said as I started out the door, "You need to be in earlier tonight."

"Why?" I asked. "You let me stay out until ten o'clock the last time."

"You owe us fifteen minutes from the last time because you

came in late. I think you need to do that as a reminder that you don't need to be late," he said in a gentle, yet authoritative voice. He was punishing me in a positive way. I learned that lesson and was never late again.

They also taught me that just because someone is not of your flesh and blood, they can become a part of you and your life. Whenever we visited any of their families (Mr. Hutchins' family in South Carolina or Mrs. Hutchins' family in Maryland), I was always included and accepted as part of the family.

Mrs. Hutchins sewed a lot during those days, and she had made new Easter dresses for Camille and me and little outfits for each of the boys. Mr. Hutchins had to make a business trip to Jacksonville, Florida, during the Easter holidays, and we all packed our bags, including our new clothes, and headed to Florida. We spent the first night in a motel in Savannah, and the next morning we were taking things out of the motel room to load the car. Mr. Hutchins had put the clothes that were on hangers in plastic bags (including our new clothes) on top of the car and returned to the room to get the luggage. When he returned to the car, someone had stolen the clothes from atop the car. We were all upset over the loss of our clothes, but they didn't allow it to spoil the fun we had on the rest of the trip. When we returned to Greeneville, Mrs. Hutchins sat down at her sewing machine and made replacement clothes for us all.

In my senior year in high school, I was chosen "Band Sponsor" for the Greeneville High School marching band, an honor that was typically a position that preformed alongside of the drum major. In a sweet way, I became a part of something of which I had no knowledge. Other than playing my guitar years earlier, I had no experience of musical instruments. I wore a uniform just like the band, and I marched with the drum major during halftime shows, parades, and special events. That year the band went to New Orleans to perform in the Sugar Bowl, as well as the Macy's Day Parade in New York, I was able to participate.

I was one of the candidates for Homecoming Queen that year. Wow! That was something for which every girl would like to be considered. Two places of honor were selected: "Homecoming

Queen" and her "Maid of Honor." I didn't care if I won. Just to be a part of it was good enough for me. I was thrilled to be selected Maid of Honor, and my special friend, Edith, was Homecoming Queen. I was nominated a "Senior Superlative" and gained the title that year of "Most Beautiful." All of these honors made me feel that I was being noticed, something I would not have admitted to but was actually craving. I no longer felt that I just existed or that I was always in the way. Greeneville High School and the community of Greeneville through Holston Methodist Home gave me a chance to be somebody. I loved them, and they seemed to love me. I could never express my gratitude enough. Greeneville became a paradise for me in so many different ways. I felt safe, cared for, and special.

During this time, my relationship with Billy ended. I grieved even though it was my decision. He called a lot, and I tried to be kind. A new interest came along; his name was Ted. He was of medium height and good looking with a terrific smile. As time went on, we began to date. He had what appeared to me to be a wonderful family, whereas Billy's were wonderful, caring, hard-working people, but there were problems that reminded me too much of where I'd been. Ted's family were church-going people—beautiful mother, handsome father, adorable little sister, and a funny, affable, crowd-pleasing younger brother, who was also nice-looking. He seemed to fit all the things I was looking for in a future mate.

Most girls were looking forward to college, making plans for a career. College was the furthest thing from my mind. I wanted what I had been robbed of since birth—a home and a family. I wanted something that no one could ever take away. I wanted my own children. In Ted, I saw that possibility. The Hutchins tried to persuade me to go to college and even assured me that Holston Home would pay my expenses. But I was determined to get married.

# CHAPTER EIGHT

On June 19, 1971, just two weeks after graduation, Ted and I were married at Christ United Methodist Church in Greeneville. The Hutchins helped me plan a beautiful wedding and gave us a lovely reception. Mr. Hutchins gave me away. It was a wonderful event. Many family and friends came to celebrate the day with us.

Each year in June, the local newspaper produced a special wedding feature. Ted and I were chosen "June Bride and Groom" that year. We were photographed with many of the local merchants, who gave us gifts and a honeymoon. How special do you think that made me feel? I felt like a princess.

Ted and I immediately settled in our new little apartment in Oak Ridge, TN about an hour and a half drive from Greeneville. Ted got a job working in the Y-12 plant for Union Carbide. I was somewhat sad, as we were no longer in that sweet comfort zone of Greeneville, but we adjusted. We came home to Greeneville at every opportunity. I can still remember the weekends we would get to come home. I would prepare a homemade pizza, pick Ted up at work, and off we would go, eating our pizza on the way. Those were good days.

Not long after we had settled, however, the Y-12 plant closed. I wasn't sad. Ted had received a job offer in Portsmouth, Virginia, with a ship builder, working night shift. We both worked at a local motel on weekend nights, managing the registration desk. We were homesick for Tennessee, family, and friends. I remember spending most of the time alone through the day because he slept. I was so bored. I tried to find things to do. There was not much to clean. We just had a bed and a kitchen table and chairs. One day I decided to paint my nails, then my toenails. When I was done, I still was in a mood to paint. That's when I looked at him lying there sleeping, and I painted his fingernails. As I completed the task, chuckling the whole time, I glanced at the clock, and then did a quick double-take. "Wake up, you're going to be late!" I yelled. He jumped up in a horrific mood, but not as horrific as when he saw his hands. He reminded me of the Incredible Hulk as he ripped his pajamas open and threw them down in a rage. I never spent my spare time doing that again.

We didn't stay in Portsmouth very long. We were soon on our way back to Tennessee. I worked several places, trying to find the right fit—a drug store, a department store. One day I ran into an old schoolmate whose father was an optometrist looking for a receptionist. I jumped on that opportunity; after all, I loved to talk. I went to work for Drs. Kelley and Parrish and worked there until January 1974. I left one day before going into the hospital to have our first child. It was a good place to work, good people. Greeneville was, and continued to be, good to me. Although I didn't know it then, I see where God was constantly intervening in my life.

When I learned that I was expecting our first child, I was so ecstatic. This was what I'd always looked forward to. I could not wait to tell everyone. My friend Elaine and I talked countless hours about the birth of our children and soon becoming mothers. Shortly after I found I was pregnant, she also became expectant. She was my friend above all friends as we went through six pregnancies together. If I wasn't pregnant, she was, and if she wasn't, I was. Those were special times, special years, and a special friendship.

In spite of the overwhelming morning sickness, each day was so exciting as I watched and then felt the changes. I was going to be a mother, and I was going to be the best mother on earth. I recall waking up one night, hearing a voice inside my head much like the one I heard after the paralyzing event of my childhood. The "voice" said to me, "This child you are carrying is more than flesh and bones, more than just a baby. It is a soul that will last forever. Everything you do and every decision you make will affect its life." Overwhelmed, I trembled, shaking the entire bed with fear. All of a sudden, I had the realization that this was not my toy. This was going to grow up to be an adult, and I was responsible for its healthy growth. I remember praying to God, "Please help me. You know I don't really know what I'm doing. Please guide me."

I was still not a Christian, but I knew God was speaking to me. Although I could have called Mrs. Hutchins, which I did on occasions, I knew she wasn't my mother. She still had three children she was trying to raise. I felt I had no one else, and God became my parent. (Years later I found God's promise to become both father and mother to those whose parents turned away. Psalms 27:10 says, "When my father and my mother forsake me, then the Lord will take me up.")

On January 15, 1974, I entered the hospital. Labor was induced on the sixteenth, and within four hours I became a mother. Immediately I was in heaven. Heather was born weighing eight pounds and fifteen ounces. Holding that little hand, caressing that little face, I knew she was a miracle. I cannot tell you how it affected me. Through every dark and lonely place in my being came sunshine. This small person belonged to me. No one could ever take her away, and I'd never leave her. She was gorgeous with dark brown hair, dark brown eyes, and dark brown skin—a female duplicate of her dad. That made me proud.

Ted's parents were wonderful people. I loved his mother, and often I would sit back and watch her be a mother to her three children. Although the years have passed since I first saw her, she is still as beautiful and loving now as she was then. I remember people saying they were the most beautiful couple in Greeneville and I certainly agreed. She has a sense of humor that would make me roll with laughter at times, but mostly because the things I was laughing about were things she never realized were funny. My children know they have a wonderful grandmother.

His dad was a very hard working, more solemn man; he stayed a lot to himself and was very private. Sometimes he would be slightly frightening just because he seemed so stern, but every now and then, I'd see a grin cross his face and with that would come a chuckle. He was part owner of a construction company that his father had started many years before. I respected him. He was a man who did what he said and expected the same from us all. He was not boastful or loud. My children adore him.

I enjoyed every minute of motherhood. Apparently, I needed to because ten-and-a-half months after Heather's birth, on December 6, we became parents again to another gorgeous little girl, Holly Anne, eight pounds and eight-and-a-half ounces. My life was busy, but I was so happy. These girls were just exactly what I needed and wanted. I felt blessed.

Mother Hutchins (I guess becoming a mother gave me an appreciation that she had been a mother to me, so I could now call her "Mother") received several calls from me. I couldn't visit her now, as they had moved to Columbia, South Carolina. One day I got a call from her that yielded more than she had expected. Both babies were sick and had been for several days. I was exhausted. When I heard her voice, I stopped long enough to sit down and cry. She talked me through it. When we hung up, I was recharged and ready to go again for another forty-eight hours.

One day when Holly was about six months old, I got a telephone call, and the voice on the other end was not familiar.

"Hi, this is your mother," the caller said.

"Excuse me?" I questioned.

"It's your mother. I thought I would like to visit. Is that okay?"

All of a sudden, the voice I hadn't heard since I was thirteen was now coming out of my phone. I didn't know what to say. I glanced at my two babies and nearly cried because I would have loved to have my mother, someone who could help me understand how to handle all the pressure of being a new mom with two new babies. I agreed to let her visit.

She visited and left. I was glad to see her go. Now divorced, she spent most of her time trying to get the attention of the single man next door. He was a disc jockey at a local radio station. It was embarrassing. She was no longer the slim, trim, pretty young lady. She wore halter tops that exposed a very large tummy covered with stretch marks. Her face was lined with the signs of the life she had lived. Apparently, she couldn't see that, or maybe she wouldn't accept the reality of aging or the life she had lived.

Life was good but busy. Ted and I bought our first home in a place called Mosheim, just a few miles outside of Greeneville. It was a sweet little ranch style house. I sold Avon, then Stanley products to help make ends meet. I loved my life. Ted did a lot with the guys while I stayed at home with the babies. Occasionally, I felt somewhat deprived of his company, but I handled it, I was always glad to believe he was having a good time and happy.

Shortly after we moved to our new home, I realized I wasn't feeling well most of the time. I finally went to the doctor, and about seven months later, on January 9, 1977, Brandon Edward was born—a healthy eight pound, thirteen-and-a-half ounce, blond-haired, blue-eyed boy. Friends teasingly dubbed him "The next fullback for the University of Tennessee." By the time he was nine months old, he weighed twenty-one pounds. The doctor ordered me to put him on a diet. He was just what Ted had always wanted, he told me.

Of course, before Brandon was born, I was ecstatic about his birth. What I didn't realize was that while I was being a mother, I was neglecting my role as wife. When I did have moments that I wasn't too tired, I would let Ted know. Apparently I had ignored him, so he totally ignored me. The entire time of my pregnancy there was absolutely no intimacy. He never smiled at me or spoke lovingly to me. I should have seen a red flag, but I trusted our love until eternity. He had become a man with whom I was unfamiliar. I cannot forget that he was young, very young; the stress of such large expectations of being the head of a family growing by leaps and a wife whose life was consumed with being a mother, is what first pushed him out of the place he originally held and into areas that resulted in him alienating himself from his family.

Sad thing was, I stayed so busy that I couldn't, or wouldn't, take time to reflect on what was happening. He had become verbally sarcastic. Looking back, I realize I should have seen that he was screaming out in his actions and words. I was just too busy to hear.

We lived in our new home for approximately eighteen months. Ted decided we would move closer to his parents, so we sold the house and moved a half block from them. I loved being near family. While in that house, he began acting very strange, saying things to me that made me cry. He made fun of everything about me, and it didn't matter if we were alone or with other people. I would run to the nearest bathroom, close the door, and cry. I was used to rejection. It was nothing new, but this time it hurt more. I just stayed busy with those blessings of mine. However, the day of reckoning was just around the corner.

That day came like a slam of ocean waves in a tsunami. This time it was different. I wasn't alone on the path of desertion; there were three others, my babies! I panicked. How was I going to do this? The fear was devastating. I can honestly say that it was unlike any I had ever known.

I called Mom and Dad Hutchins. I stayed with them in Columbia for two weeks and then went back home to Greeneville. I filed for divorce. I couldn't bear the anticipated pain of him telling me he wanted to leave, so I took control and helped him.

I'll never forget what he told me. "I used to be first in your life, but the children have taken my place. I am jealous." He also added that he was tired of seeing me pregnant, to which I responded that I was tired of being pregnant, but there was nothing I could do about it. I look back with deep regret, knowing what my inattention did to our home. It certainly wasn't on purpose. In my desire to be the best mother, I guess I forgot about being a good wife.

I can honestly say that I deeply loved him when we divorced. I now realize I acted on fear—fear of the past when everyone in my life had the upper hand. They had always left me. Not this time! I made the decision that I had to leave him before he left me. Somehow it seemed less painful that way.

Ted went his way and I went mine. Although he pleaded for reconciliation, I turned a deaf ear. We both dated. His dating was healthier than mine. When I realized it wasn't healthy, I decided reuniting was better. I called him, but his exact words were, "I'm happier than I've ever been."

I feel sad that the end of my marriage to Ted brought his mother tears and his father pain. I hope they have forgiven me for that.

# Chapter Nine

I found myself alone and dreading the future. I began hoping for someone who would love my children and love me unconditionally, someone who would take care of all of us, someone in church. That was a priority because I thought people in church were good.

There was a gentleman who spoke with me often at my job, a job Ted had insisted before I learned of his indiscretions, I get because I wasn't "earning my keep." He told me if I worked in the evenings, he would take care of three children—Brandon was less than a year old. It was hard for me, but I honored my husband's wishes. I soon discovered that he eventually hired a babysitter. I eventually realized it was all to give him his freedom.

This man always showed up at my workplace and seemed to have an interest in me even before Ted and I divorced. At first, I couldn't stand him. He seemed like a flirt (Red Flag #1, eventually ignored). Everyone was talking about what a wonderful person he was and how good he was to children. He told me he had been married but was in the midst of divorce (Red Flag #2, ignored). One day he asked me to meet him for lunch, not in Greeneville, but in Newport (Red Flag #3, caused me to stop and think, but then ignored). *What's the problem with going to lunch with someone?* I rationalized. *He's already in the process of a divorce, just like me. Past relationships are over. What's the big deal?* I convinced myself it was okay, and so I went. Over lunch, he said he wanted to talk with me more but not around so many people. I remember feeling a bit sick, but I said okay. Wrong move. He already had a hotel room waiting. He had planned more than a talk.

I told him that I was not that kind of woman, to which he responded, "I know that. Do you think I would be interested in you if you were? I have watched you for a long, long time, and when everything is over with Ted, I want you, if you'll have me."

I didn't realize what sly dogs look like, but I do now. He was one! I was, on one hand, feeling wanted, but on the other hand, Ted had been my whole life for so long. He had been the only person who had touched me in eight years. But I fell into the trap set for me. My life would go down hill from there, further than I could have ever imagined a life could go and still survive. Everything that I had experienced before was mild, because now I could make decisions, and the ones I made were lifelong scars, deeper than any I had from my prior life, and I would wear them forever.

Donald was seventeen years older than me, wealthy, and loved to flaunt it. I was intrigued with his confessions of what God had done in his life. Being the confused person that I was, I kept thinking, *This could be good! I can take care of my children, I won't have to work, he goes to church, and he believes in God. Okay*, I told myself. *Maybe I don't feel the way I did about Ted, but maybe it will grow with time. Plus, he is older, I am younger—maybe he'll never need another woman, much less a younger woman. I already am a younger woman.*

I continued to see Donald. He convinced me to move to another city to begin a new life. Only later did I realize that he was attempting to keep our relationship secret. My life was not good. I couldn't get a job that paid me enough to put the children in daycare, and I was forced to accept public assistance. I had a car that often was not in running order, so I regularly walked with Heather to kindergarten in the morning and back in the evening with Brandon on my hip—a half mile each way. Donald gave me no financial assistance. Whenever I attempted to end the relationship, he would always paint this perfect picture of how it was going to be. I fell for it—hook, line, and sinker. I can honestly say I didn't love him. I cared for him and thought I would never love again like I loved Ted. I thought this was the next best thing.

The children and I lived in a house far from friends and the children's grandparents. After two years, I longed to see my friends in Greeneville and to be nearer the children's grandparents. I found an apartment across the street from my friend Carolyn and her children in Greeneville. I was so happy, the children's grandparents were happy, and my children were happy. I was still seeing Donald—still not divorced, but constantly telling me they were "still negotiating." His reasoning was he had so much money and so many businesses.

One day there was a knock at my door. I opened the door and recognized Donald's soon-to-be ex-wife. As I opened the door, she propped her foot inside and began to let me know, in her terms, what she thought of my character. As I stood there and listened, I realized everything she said was right, and I hated it. I told her I was very sorry, and if their marriage could be mended, that was the best thing. What hurt me most was that my three little children were standing behind me as she said things that led me to evaluate what kind of person I was. It wasn't a pretty picture.

"You've said what you've come here to say, and I understand, but I believe it's time for you to go," I said, leaving no room for a continuance. However, as she stepped away, she began again. "Donald and I have never considered divorce!" She paused momentarily and then continued, "But if you think you're the first, think again. If you think you'll be the last, you need to know that *you're a fool.*"

I felt like trash! I didn't just feel like a really bad person, I knew I was. Why would he lie and tell me their marriage was over? Again I had been betrayed, but this time I deserved it. I should have realized two years was a bit long, but somehow he convinced me she was fighting for more, which kept the divorce from becoming final.

Later that day, Donald came over. I told him about his wife's visit, and he assured me that her words were lies. She was just angry because he had already found someone. I wanted to believe, so I did. I was so confused.

I thought, *If I had forgiven Ted when he first asked, I would not be living like this.* I felt terrible. It couldn't get any worse. I wanted nothing to do with this relationship anymore. When Ted had often asked me to reconcile, I was not ready to forgive him. Again I got up the courage to ask him; he was kind, but he turned me down again and added that he had never been happier. He was in a relationship that was the one he had been looking for. My heart broke. I continued to sob, not just cry. I got what I deserved. Several months later Ted was married. I especially remember that day. I was home alone. The children were at their father's wedding. As the wedding party passed near my house, horns were blowing in celebration. I remember lying on my back in the floor of my living room, praying for God to help me heal.

Things were spiraling downhill. My intimate relationship was the part that bothered me most. I felt wrong about it. At times, I thought it seemed that everyone else was involved that way, so why was I feeling so guilty? It was out of character for me and I knew it, but I wanted to be loved so much that I would do nearly anything.

The time came when I realized I was sick. I'd felt it before. I cried out to God after a doctor confirmed I was pregnant. This was the darkest time of my life, even to this day. I could blame no one but myself. I told the doctor my dilemma. I had three children, and their father might seek custody of the children if he knew. The fear of losing my children was so great that I couldn't think straight. The doctor told me that it was only a mass of tissue at that point. It wasn't a baby yet, and if I did something quickly, it would be like having a dilatation and curettage, which is a medical procedure that usually follows a miscarriage, which he believed could happen because my body was seeping fluid. That led him to the diagnosis that my body was probably going to abort naturally. My body wasn't healthy enough to carry the baby, and I would be saving myself an inevitable situation. I breathed a sign of relief. He told me everything I needed to know not to have a guilty conscience, I thought. But hardly a day passes that I don't think about what that relationship incurred. The D&C, which actually was a termination of pregnancy commonly known as an abortion, didn't seem right to do, but when I told Donald, he didn't hesitate to give me the money I needed. I found it strange that he would never buy as much as a McDonald's meal for the children, but he didn't blink twice about this. I felt I had no choice. This was the most difficult chapter of my life, without reservation. I had a regret that was overwhelming; except for God's Grace, I could not have faced the abortion as the years went by or the next life-altering event. It was a daily reminder to me. You would have thought I would have learned something by now, but I hadn't.

Six months later, I went back to see the same doctor for my second "D&C." This time I didn't just cry, I screamed in excruciating sorrow. From the very depth of my being came groans so loud that the doctor thought I was in physical pain. I'm sure it affected him. His nurse told him I was grieving, and she certainly had that figured correctly.

Something was very, very wrong with my life and I knew it. The only thing I could think of was that maybe going to church would help me. However, my car was not in running condition, so I had to choose a church near where I lived. Sunday morning came, and the children and I walked half a mile to First Baptist Church in Greeneville. We went up in the balcony to sit. As I looked down, my eyes welled with tears. There sat three women who had befriended me. Helen Cleek (affectionately called "Cookie" by family and friends) sat on the left side. She had been a house parent at Holston Home who took a special interest in the children, especially us girls. She pierced my ears when I was fifteen, took me shopping, and to the movies. I loved her.

Then there was Alice McDaniels, who had witnessed to me around the age of eighteen when we worked together stocking a department store for opening. We had a manager whose tongue delivered some pretty foul language. When he profaned God's name, I cringed simply because I knew it was wrong but didn't have the conviction in my life to say anything at the point. One day as I was working with Alice, our "boss" used offensive language that degraded the Father God. Alice stopped working and said to him, "You know, that is my heavenly Father and He deserves respect. Please don't disrespect him by using His name that way." I remember thinking, *This will be her last day!* He looked at her for a moment and said, "Okay, Mom, let's get back to work." I never heard him use that language again, but from that day on he called her "Mom." It was a witness of strength, conviction, and healthy belief. I've always admired her, especially because of that day.

I saw Helen Rollins, who is now Helen Rollins Sorrells, at the piano. I had worked with Helen before the birth of my first child,

Heather. I saw something very different in her, unlike anything I had ever witnessed in a workplace. We worked with about ten other people, mostly women, but Helen stood out. She was a wife, a mother of two daughters, Debbie and Donna. She was just so special, kind, considerate, a wonderful example of a mother, and Christian (although I didn't think about the latter at the time). I wanted to be just like her. Helen was the person I had gone to when I chose to leave Ted. She told me then, "People make mistakes. Your children need their father. No one will ever love them like their father."

Of course, I didn't listen. No matter where I was, no matter what I did, Helen always cared about me. Almost every time I saw her she would tell me she had been praying for me. I thank God for Helen. She was and still is such a godly example. As I looked at her sitting there, I realized why she was different. God was central in her life. I also realized that the wish I had to be like her was definitely never going to happen. I had already gone too far.

As I sat in church, looking at these three women who had impacted my life, I got a shocking dose of reality. *Where have I been, where am I now, and where am I going with my life?*

I went home after church, and the impact of that Sunday morning was so explosive that it erupted like a volcano of wonderful feelings and the desire to search for God. I wanted and needed to know His Word. I studied and studied and studied. I read the Bible in the mornings and took care of the children, then at nap time I studied more. I watched Christians on television.

Then one day, while watching the "700 Club," I gave my heart to Jesus. After I watched and heard just what God intended me to hear that day, Ben Kinchlow, co-host of the program, placed his hand on the screen and asked me to place my hand with his as he prayed. Somehow I knew he was talking directly to me. I knelt in front of the TV, placed my hand on the screen over the top of Ben Kinchlow's, and repeated "The Sinner's Prayer." It was the most amazing feeling that ever happened to me. All of a sudden, it felt like something was being poured slowly over the crown of my head, down my shoulders, and onto my trunk. I didn't understand then, but as I shared that event with my pastor, he smiled and told me it was the Holy Spirit coming to live in me. I cried.

After that experience, I joined the church. That was one of the greatest days of my life. I had a family—a really big family. They loved me, they loved my children, and I loved them. It also made me have second thoughts about my relationship with Donald. What was so ironic is that Donald had been the first person to explain in detail to me about Jesus and his purpose for our lives. That's one reason I was attracted to him. As I look back, I realize others showed me Jesus by example, Donald only spoke words.

Although Donald was divorced by that time, I began questioning my relationship with him. Satan's lies would come as, "Who else would accept you with three children?" or "You've already started a life with him. What will the children think if he's no longer around and someone else comes in? How mixed up will that be for them?" or "You'll be alone again." I allowed Satan's urging to overshadow what I knew was right and good, and I continued with him and a life straight from the gut of torment. But this time I can blame no one but myself. The only thing that sustained me was the love for my children, my love for Jesus, a daily Bible study, and the support of my church. But with all that, I still allowed the fear of being alone to control my actions when it came to relationships. I made a choice and I would stay with it.

Donald was still pursuing an intimate relationship, but I wanted to live better and told him exactly that. He told me that when you plan on getting married, it's okay. Something told me that it wasn't. I went to consult with my pastor, and he confirmed my conviction; now I knew God's standards of right and wrong. I should do the right thing and refuse Donald. It wasn't hard this time to look at him and tell him he was wrong. Soon Donald started going to church with me. Still questioning, I would pray to God, "If Donald is not for me, please show me." I believed then as I do now God actually did show me. Several things happened to enlighten me, but because of fear, I ignored them, and the question always lingered, "Was that really God or just me thinking it?" I had asked God for help, but I didn't heed it. I got what I deserved. Satan took advantage of my fear.

I tried to be what I should be at all times; however, I wasn't perfect by any stretch of the word, but when I failed, I felt the gentle nudging of the Holy Spirit. I would pray for forgiveness and continue to grow closer to God.

I recall the first real time I honored the voice of the Lord in an act of faith. I was sitting in the pew to the back of the church on the left side, near the aisle. It was time to take the offering; however, I wasn't going to give anything because all I had was seventy-eight cents. However, God had another plan; his voice spoke to me and said, *Give.*

I was startled and responded in my mind, *But all I have is seventy-eight cents!* Next, I heard, *Give it all.*

*What?* was my response with disbelief.

*Give it all.* And with that, I did. I didn't look up at the usher as he passed the plate for fear of him looking at me thinking, *Ah come on!* But it felt good. I knew I had honored God in faith. That very week, I had a knock on my door. I answered it, and there stood three men and a couch, *no kidding*! I believed that they needed directions to some other tenant's apartment. I smiled and asked them if I could help them. They smiled pleasantly and asked, "Are you Rita?"

Startled, I said, "Yes!"

"We're supposed to deliver this to you," one of the men said.

"What? I didn't order this," I said nervously.

"This is a gift from someone who wants to remain anonymous," he said.

"Are you kidding?" I responded in disbelief.

"No, it's really yours!"

I watched as those same men carried out my old couch with springs protruding out of it, much like the one I slept on as a very small child. You can't out give God. I got that new beautiful couch for seventy-eight cents. To this day I do not know from what human that couch came, but I know who sent it.

Donald and I were married on August 7, 1981. What I got was exactly what God knew and wanted to keep me from: a marriage with a man who was manipulating, self-centered, egotistical, self-serving, and mostly a liar. He could—and did—eat steaks in front of my children and never blink while we ate Spam.

Six months into our marriage, I learned I was expecting another baby. He immediately told me to get an abortion. I remember looking at him in disbelief. "I can't do that, I'm a Christian now!" holding the tears back. "If you don't, I will walk out the door and never look back!" he stormed "But I'm a Christian didn't you hear me! I can't do that. It's wrong!" I pleaded

"I didn't marry you to have children," he stormed. "We have enough. Tomorrow you *will* check on it!"

The next day I went to see the pastor who had married us. I told him my situation. He told me if I were his daughter and had asked him before I married Donald, he would have told me to run. But he added, "You're not my daughter. However, you are married to him. He is the head of your house, he is responsible, and you must do what he says. He will be the one that pays ultimately." Next, I went to my doctor, who had just gone from Sunday school teacher to agnostic. He would always smile a genuine smile and give me a hug when I would ask him if I could continue to pray for him; he always said yes.

I appreciate Dr. Hoppe. Even though he was not a Christian (by his own admission) at that time in his life, he still pointed me in the right direction. Without his guidance, I would not have Synthia. I told Dr. Hoppe of my dilemma.

"Because of your situation, I know of facilities that might take care of you. They are often used for cases of incest or rape; however, I will have to check. I'm just not sure."

"What should I do?" I asked him.

"The easiest thing to do would be to have an abortion and get it over with."

"But Dr. Hoppe, you don't understand. I don't want to do the easy thing. I want to do the right thing."

"In that case," he said without pause, "you'll have your baby."

That's exactly what I wanted someone to say. It still brings tears to my eyes when I recall his words. I knew he was right. The counsel of the godly said to do it, and the counsel of the godless said not to. What's wrong with that picture? (I do believe the pastor/counselor did eventually change his position on that issue, which proved that we all continue to grow and learn if we pray and seek God's guidance. I still love that pastor. He was with me through so much in so many different aspects of my life, helping me immensely.)

The pregnancy was difficult and long. Donald turned his back to me every night and would not talk to me, much like Ted did with my last pregnancy with him. Donald would get up in the mornings, leave the house without speaking, and not come home until late at night. His days were spent at a shopping mall, walking, talking, and apparently flirting.

The only words he would speak to me were, "Are you going today?"

I finally had the courage, after much prayer, to tell him, "I will not. I am not! I realize I am the only person living who will protect my baby's life. I will do the right thing this time. So should you choose to leave me, please do it now, not when I have a baby in my arms."

I couldn't believe I said it, but I knew that through God I was strong enough. It felt good to do the right thing no matter what the cost.

I had spent weeks and weeks on end so depressed that I could hardly get out of bed. I functioned enough to take care of my children, but that was all. I hated that I had to open my eyes and see through the windows of the dawning day. For me it was a dawning of another day of sorrow and pain. I sought God's love and peace. I remember waking up and wishing that I hadn't. My spiritual life was existing in the tears I cried daily, and my earthly life was not a good witness. I wanted to sleep through it all. I remember being concerned, *If he leaves, how will I ever feed my children*? Not that Donald ever supplied any groceries, but I realized that he did supply a roof over our heads. If he left, I would have to supply that roof. I decided one way to make sure my baby was fed was to become a nursing mother when being a nursing mother wasn't cool. I knew this *was* the right thing, and I also knew I would lose everything except my children. It didn't matter, God would supply. I acted on faith, and for the first time in my life, I stood firm and did not budge. My baby was a gift and special, just as special as all my other children. I had to fight for his or her life. I may not have won many battles, but that one I did.

As I looked back prior to our marriage, Donald had seemed to care about my children, although I realize in retrospect that he never took them anywhere, never spent any money on them, and always seemed to be on hand at meal times. I realized, too late, that I was made to support myself and my children and now I was feeding Donald on the payments from my ex-husband, which, of course, was for the three children. Donald was contributing absolutely nothing to the family, except a roof. I kept expecting him to change, I prayed for him to change. God knew his heart; again, he had tried to warn me.

During this time of my deep depression, I had to go next door to call my ex-mother-in-law, because Donald wouldn't put a phone in the house. I asked her if she would come and visit me. When she did, I was so sick in bed that she sat in a chair next to me. She listened to my pleas as I cried to her, "I'm probably going to be raising this baby on my own. Please don't take the other children away. I know I won't have a job and probably won't have much to live on, but please don't take them. They are my life." She sat there, looked at the pitiful state I was in, and said, "I would never try to take the children away. They may not have a lot and even less to look forward to, but I know that you love them and they will have that, for sure. I will help every way I can." Those were the words I needed to hear to give me strength to get up and get started again. As I look back, I see again where fear was one of the biggest demons in my life. I still fight it. For reasons I'm not certain, Donald never left.

During my pregnancy, Donald would not allow me to wear maternity clothes to church or in any public place. I had to hide my pregnancy as though it was shameful. I was told not to tell anyone. Of course, there came a time when it no longer could be hidden.

From time to time, his ex-wife would visit us. Often she would just come to my door and bang, scream, and bang some more. I never answered the door. I watched her leave once and she stopped at my mailbox and left something. After she was gone, I went to the mailbox and got the note, which, to my surprise, read, "Aren't you even the least bit curious as to where your husband is late at night? He is with me, just like last night and tonight."

I was sick, pregnant, and lonely. When I confronted him, he denied her accusations as he had the first time she made the same accusations years before. Finally, at the urging of a business associate, he had a phone installed, but I would soon regret that decision.

His ex-wife made several more visits to our house. When she would come, the children would hide in their closets, frightened by her screaming and banging. She visited once or twice more and then totally stopped. That's when the phone calls and messages about my unfaithful husband began. I could blame no one but myself. It was no less than I deserved.

I would take out my Bible daily, sit in the backyard under a low-limbed dogwood tree, and read aloud. While I read, I would rub my stomach, hoping that somehow my baby would feel my hands of love for her and hear God's Words, I prayed those words would make a difference in her life.

One afternoon while sitting under that tree, watching the children play in their wading pool, a motorcycle drove up in the backyard. I was startled because I had no idea who was under that helmet. When he removed his helmet, I was surprised to see Ted. He smiled and said, "I've come to apologize for everything I did to you. You didn't deserve any of it."

All I could say was, "That's okay."

Just as quickly as he appeared, he put on his helmet and left. I felt special in an odd sort of way. He had recognized the wrong done and rectified it by an apology without giving me the opportunity to take any blame.

I told Donald that evening when he finally came home, and it made him angry. He said Ted was just trying to "weasel his way back" into my life. I reminded him that I was pregnant and didn't think that was what Ted had in mind at all; I knew it was real and honest.

I gave birth to my baby Synthia, eight pounds and ten-and-a-half ounces on November 19, 1982. She was special. I would look at her and realize that I had come a long way. She was evidence of that. She was living and breathing. My friends Helen Rollins, Helen's daughters, Debbie and Donna, and "Cookie" were there, as was Donald. Dr. Hoppe helped deliver Synthia for the *second time*. All these people were crucial to her existence. Helen and Cookie had helped me through some very difficult times. I love them.

A few days after Synthia's birth, Donald did apologize for asking me to terminate the pregnancy; I believe his exact words were, "I'm glad you didn't listen to me that time."

It was healing. I wanted to believe everything would be all right from then on. But it wasn't.

For sixteen long, hard years I held on in constant prayer. As I remember, the cruelty and abuse began as early as two weeks after our marriage. That's when he alerted me that he would not be responsible for any of my needs. If they were met, I was to take it out of the children's support money. (I thank God that Ted was faithful to support our children, and I knew I could count on those checks to arrive on time each month.) I reminded Donald that it was money to take care of the children and not for me.

His response was, "You can use that or you'll do without." For many years I did just that—*went without*. He wouldn't give me money for groceries but told me to use their money. What infuriated me most about that was that he ate too.

So many times I wanted to walk out, but I couldn't. Donald made certain I had no money, but I would always remember that not only did I take an oath to my husband, but it was a covenant with God. I adjusted and went on. As I studied and grew to understand the Scriptures, I realized God's blueprints for how we are supposed to live are in the Scriptures. Obviously, before I married Donald I hadn't read enough. Through all of my tribulations and knowing that I was paying a price for not heeding God's Word, I still felt the presence of God. I learned a lot the hard way.

The cars I had to drive were nice to look at but always had some mechanical defect. This was a mirror image of the way Donald lived his life. He looked good on the outside but the inside was dysfunctional. Donald was a "fly-by-night" used car salesman, along with many other things he dabbled in (most of which he kept from me). He always drove new, top-of-the-line vehicles—Lincolns, Cadillacs, or Lexuses—while the family was lucky to get one that started with a key.

Once when Synthia was an infant, I went shopping at a local grocery store. The only way to start the car was to open the hood and put a screwdriver down between the starter and something else (I didn't know the names of car parts; I just knew where to put the screwdriver). On this particular day I had put all of the children back into the car, Heather, nine, Holly, eight, Brandon, six, and newborn Synthia. I went around the car with my screwdriver and proceeded to make the usual contact I needed in order to start the engine. When it started, it immediately took off and brushed my body, nearly knocking me down. I screamed as I ran after the car when a gentleman rushed to our rescue, jumped into the car, and stopped it. Thankfully, I had left the door open, but I had also left the car in gear. I couldn't thank him enough, but I wanted to kill Donald. I was glad I was a Christian!

The cars were one issue, but our home was another. Our first home was a three bedroom, two-story house in a nice area just on the outskirts of Greeneville. The owners were getting a divorce, and Donald figured they would take a substantial loss just to sell it. He was right. The house looked good from the outside and the inside seemed okay. My friend Carolyn and her family helped me to paint and hang wallpaper. She often helped me with groceries when things got low, and I had no source of getting any. I treasure her friendship.

As winter approached, I noticed a major problem. The house had ceiling heat, and only one room in the house would heat. That room was the master bedroom. The children's rooms were so cold in the winter that I would make them pallets on the floor in my room. Donald would get angry and tell me that I was baby-ing them too much. When I asked him to please fix the heat in the rest of the house so they could sleep in their own rooms, he'd tell me there was nothing wrong, that it was warm enough, and besides, it would cost too much.

Even though Donald, by his own admission, was a wealthy man, he would not so much as buy a gallon of milk for his own baby. If he did buy anything, it was always for himself. As he would bring his "goodies" into the house, he would carry them proudly in front of the entire family, up the steps, and to his bedroom where he hid them where the children could not reach them.

One day the mailman delivered a notice from the power company that our bill was overdue and the electricity would be cut off. Somehow I found a blank check from Donald's checking account and paid the bill. After several days, my conscience began to bother me, so I confessed to him what I had done.

He said, "When will you be able to repay me the $168?" He reminded me of that "debt" frequently for months thereafter.

I would have to dress for winter just to go downstairs to the kitchen. I could never take the baby downstairs, so we lived in my bedroom. I distinctly remember often picking up drinking glasses that were left in the sink from the night before and they would have water frozen in them. Fortunately, the older children were in school, so they would be warm in the daytime hours.

Donald had the ability to lure people in, making them believe things that were to his advantage. That's what he did best, besides delivering mental blows that never showed outside bruising but strangled your very desire to live.

An instance that pretty well described the degree of his lack of concern for my needs was when I asked if I could buy a new slip. During my pregnancy, I had worn the same slip I had prior to my pregnancy, and it had lost all its elasticity.

His response was, "Can you afford it?"

Of course, I couldn't and said, "No."

He looked at me with a smirk and said, "Oh, well!" as he walked away.

He boasted of being worth 2.5 million dollars, but he wouldn't pay a light bill for his family. He often spoke about how good the steak he ate for lunch was, while I was scrambling through the cabinets to find something for our supper. Once, however, I must have caught him in a generous mood. I showed him the bare shelves in the cabinets and said, "We don't even have a loaf of bread!"

He put his hand in his pocket and asked, "How much does a loaf of bread cost?"

I responded, "Eighty-three cents." He counted exactly eighty-three cents and handed it to me. I had forgotten about the sales tax. I dug through the car, pockets, couch, and chairs for the remaining change.

My ex-mother-in-law was kind to me and wonderful to the children. She often passed clothes down to me. Without her, I would have had little or nothing to wear. She and her husband, the children's grandfather, made sure the children had all the necessities. They took the children every other weekend to visit them, took them on vacation, and made them feel very special. I thank God for them.

On Sundays after church, the children would often asked to go to McDonald's like their friends. Donald always whined, "It costs too much!"

Inside I cried all the time; inside my children cried all the time. I finally started putting change that I would find lying here and there in a jar that I kept hidden. When I had enough, I'd cash it in for bills and gave the children money on Sunday so we could go to McDonald's.

He would ask where they got their money, and I would just say, "It's their money." I found a way for my children to have Sunday at McDonald's just like other families.

I know a lot of readers will be angrier at me for staying than at him. I realize it's hard to understand, but I had not only taken a vow to Donald and to God to live with him "until death do you part," but the admission of failure was overwhelming. I was alone; I didn't have a mother to run home to. I did the best I could with the choices that were available. The thought of starting over with the children just made me believe this was better than a life of stark poverty such as I had known before. At least we had a place to live. I just kept praying it would get better.

I often realized that because of the way he treated the children and me, any "love" that had developed over time for him was gone.

I knew in order to withstand this life I had to feel love for him, so I pleaded with God to let me love him. I prayed this prayer over and over through the years. I reasoned that God honored my request. Suddenly, I would feel love for him; however, it was a love that was laced daily with painful moments.

Once, while the older children were visiting their grandparents, Donald took Synthia and me to spend the weekend in Gatlinburg, Tennessee. God only knows how guilty I felt, I could never take all of my children anywhere. As we were having an evening meal, a lady approached us and inquired about Synthia. She noticed the fact that she was a very happy, friendly child of seventeen months. She explained that she was a scout for a modeling agency in Knox-ville, and the agency had been looking for a young child like her to train for an upcoming bridal fair. The next week we took Synthia for an interview with the owner of the agency. We took the other children with us. As the lady approached us, she looked at all the children and asked if they were all there for an interview, to which Donald quickly said, "No."

She stood looking at them and said, "I'm telling you guys, they should be. They are gorgeous."

Synthia was the only one who ended up in the bridal fair, but all the girls eventually became child models in New York City for an agency known as Rascals of Manhattan. Brandon had absolutely no interest, but he did become the most envied boy at school. Every boy wanted to come home with him.

Donald provided the funds up front for trips to New York. He was, after all, a business man. The girls worked from the day we got there until the day we left, earning excellent money. We returned to the city in the spring of the next year. We sub-leased an apartment in Manhattan. The girls worked constantly. Heather, Holly, and Synthia appeared in advertisements in major maga-zines and newspapers: *Woman's World*, ads for Zayre's and Fisher-Price, just to name a few. We spent two weeks the first trip and six weeks the next. I soon realized the children were working for Donald. He had chosen to take every check they made and pocket it. I was agreeable to reimbursing his expenses, but the children never received one dime from all the work they did. I couldn't let that continue, so I ended their modeling career. He had used us enough. I'll never forget my childhood friend, Catherine, who commented that the children and I were great tax deductions for Donald. It took me many years before I realized that what she said was exactly what we were. Nothing more!

Shortly after we returned from New York, Donald's elderly mother became very ill and passed away. At the same time, Donald was having a great deal of trouble with his ex-wife. She sued him for additional support for their youngest daughter. He told me she had taken him to court once before we got married to raise the child support and for more money for keeping his books. Keeping his books? I asked him why she was still keeping his books. He explained that she knew how he liked them done and understood how he did things. I was furious. Maybe that's why she stayed so angry. He still had her on the hook.

He began hiding monies and moving his assets around. He always carried a locked briefcase. We made several trips to a bank in South Carolina, where he would go into the bank while I sat in the car. As I waited, I wondered what he was doing. He always reasoned that he was cashing a check. After several trips to the same out-of-state bank, I became somewhat inquisitive and followed him into the bank. He then confessed that his ex-wife was demanding more of his money, and that she had gotten all she was going to get. I realized then he was hiding money from her.

What I didn't know at the time was that he had talked Mom Hutchins into signing for the safe-deposit box since she was a resident, and he put a substantial amount of assets in the box. He even used her Social Security number to open it. What neither she nor I knew until the box rent became due a year later was that on those trips he was slyly removing things from the box. When she went to pay the rent, bank personnel told her the box had been emptied and closed.

I was living in such a ridiculous world. I put myself in his ex-wife's place and, knowing what a miser he was—and knowing he didn't become one overnight—I told him, "She was your wife for a long time. She gave birth to two of your children. She worked hard to keep your books, and she worked outside the home. If she deserves more, you need to give it to her."

He responded, "She only worked when she wanted to, and I've already paid her back for what she brought home. No court, no judge, no government, nobody is going to tell me how to spend *my* money."

Shortly after those trips, he filed bankruptcy, and our home went up for auction. Years later, I found documents where he had made land deals and used my children's names and Social Security numbers. He even had my brother Johnny's name and Social Security number, as well as several friends on land deals he had made.

Heather and Holly did well in school. They were very popular and became cheerleaders. Remembering my own high school years, I was happy for them, but with scarcely enough money to feed them, I wondered how I was going to buy their outfits. Their dad came to the rescue this time. Brandon, being a boy, got into trouble every now and then. I reasoned that the teachers were just picking on him because he was a good boy! I made excuses for him until he borrowed the car—a Ford Mustang that Donald had bought for re-sale. Brandon was only thirteen. He went to town and picked up all his friends and chauffeured them around. He decided to stop at a convenience store, where he met a cousin. She told on him! Brandon didn't deny it and took his restriction. We never left the keys just hanging around again.

One day Donald told me abruptly that we had to leave town and settle somewhere else.

"Where?" I asked.

"Somewhere no one will know, where you can never call home again"

"What?" I asked. "Why? That's not possible. The children have to talk with their grandparents."

"No, not even the children's grandparents."

He told me of a plan he had to borrow a large sum of money from the bank and disappear.

Infuriated, I said very firmly, "I cannot do that. First, it's wrong, and I won't do that to my children or their grandparents. My children love their grandparents and they love my children. It would kill them."

"Then you'll have to give the children to them!" he responded.

"I will never, ever give my children away!" I said, not believing what I'd just heard.

He said, "One way or the other! You make the decision."

"I have made my decision and neither of those is it," I responded. I surprised myself. I always tried to be submissive, but this was one of those times he was crossing the line and I stood firm against him.

After I took my stand, he decided the only other option was to move into his mother's house. He didn't stay behind because he loved me. He didn't stay behind because I was firm. He stayed behind because he was uneducated. He needed assistance to go beyond the territory with which he was familiar. He could not read directions, and he could not read signs. Sometimes I wonder if that wasn't why he did some of the drastic things he did—to ensure he kept the same lifestyle he was used to living, whether by stealing or using others. Could he have possibly suffered from fear, as I did?

I cared for his elderly, mentally challenged brother, Micah. Micah was a special person, kind and quiet. He was about six-years-old mentally, but had a memory that was unbelievable. He could tell you what the weather had been twenty years ago on any given date. He reminded me of the part Dustin Hoffman played in the movie *Rain Man*. The children learned to love him and so did I.

Micah had not had the opportunity to leave home much. He would go to church and walk home. I wanted to make his life better. He had lost all his teeth and his hearing was very bad. I had him fitted with dentures and he was so proud. I often found him looking in the mirror at himself, grinning. One night I took him to our church for a supper. He decided he could eat better without his new teeth. He took them out of his mouth and laid them beside his plate. I nearly jumped out of my skin. I quickly took a napkin and covered them and put them in my purse. I heard a few chuckles around us.

I also sought information on having his hearing restored by a surgical procedure that rebuilt his ear drums. He was covered by a state insurance plan that covered the operation. After he came home, he had a hard time sleeping, as he said he heard traffic all night long.

He never had a television until we moved into the house with him. After we got the television hooked up, he was so taken by what he saw that he watched it constantly. After the first night I asked him how he had slept that night.

"Not too good," he said.

"Why?" I asked.

"I was watchin' that there TV and saw all them people gettin' killed. I ain't never seen anyone get killed before."

I assured him that it was just a movie and not real. He was relieved.

After we moved into his and Donald's home place in the country, Donald decided to remodel it. His siblings didn't have a problem with it since I had taken the responsibility of caring for Micah. All of them felt they were too old to handle caring for him. The family agreement was that Donald would not have to purchase the home until two years after Micah died. We could just live there for nothing so long as we took care of Micah.

Donald had a deed drawn up for the ownership of the farm in contemplation of buying the house and the one-hundred-acre farm as the agreement stated some two years of Micah's death. In the process of doing this, he discovered that a half-brother who lived in California was heir to a portion of it. The siblings had the same father, but the brother's mother had died along with a child due to the influenza epidemic of that time. Donald's mother was his father's second wife. When Donald realized his half-brother's name was on the new deed, he brought it to me to forge his brother's name on the release. I refused, telling him I would not steal someone's birthright, that if it got done he would have to do it. Angry as he was, I did not budge.

Donald brought in a "land appraiser" who was also a friend of his. His siblings had no idea of what the place was worth. They trusted him, and he took advantage of their trust. The house, before Donald remodeled it, was worth at least forty-five thousand to fifty thousand dollars without the land. Donald told them the house and land together appraised for forty-five thousand. I told him he was taking advantage of his brothers and sisters. His nine siblings weren't poor, but most of them certainly didn't have any extra. After he divided forty-five thousand dollars between ten, each sibling received about forty-five hundred dollars. He had no problem sleeping, but his deception caused me many sleepless nights.

Another advantage for Donald was that the farm had no debt, thus no payments. He also realized that Micah received a monthly Social Security check. He ordered me to use it to pay all the household bills and buy groceries. Six hundred dollars a month didn't go very far, but it certainly was more than the two hundred dollars I was receiving for child support. But now that Micah's money was available, Donald told me that I had to pay the power bill, groceries, and anything else it took to run the house as I always had, but now expenses were more, gas, groceries and a huge home's electricity bill besides caring for one more person. The three older children would soon be in high school and there was nothing inexpensive about that. He didn't as much as buy his own drinks, and when I did, he hid them in his closet and locked it. No child was going to get his drinks!

Although Donald remodeled the house at a cost of eighty thousand dollars, he never paid for nor bought another thing after that. Of course, he had to appear on the outside how he wanted people to believe he lived. It was very important that the world viewed him as a wealthy man. The funny part was, Donald had an elementary education, proclaimed to be a self-made man, and on occasion when he wanted to impress a clergy person or someone who was a Christian, he would say, "The Lord has blessed me with the ability to make money."

Often, he would look at me when I would doubt something he would propose to do and asked, "Who has God given the ability to make money? How many apples are in your cart?" I never responded. I'd just walk away.

One of the saddest days in that house was the day Micah asked me for a new pair of shoes. Micah never asked for anything, but he held up his shoe for me to see the hole in the sole. I almost cried. "You'll get new shoes," I told him.

When Donald came home, I told him of Micah's need, and his reply was, "Where does he go to need new shoes? He doesn't need new shoes!"

I couldn't believe a man with thirty pairs of shoes in his closet could honestly deprive his own mentally challenged brother of a pair of new shoes. Apparently, Micah had heard the conversation. I found him crying. I consoled him and told him he would have a new pair of shoes as soon as I could get them. I kept my promise.

I also recall what Donald said when I told him that Synthia, his own four-year-old daughter, needed a new pair of shoes. "She'll just grow out of them. It's wasted money." I tried very hard not to, but it was becoming real easy to hate him.

In 1987, I received word that my adoptive mother was gravely ill. On the occasion of a visit several years earlier, we had made peace with each other. She had asked for my forgiveness, and I had granted it. On that same visit I had a wonderful experience of leading her into a personal relationship with Jesus, which was followed by a neighbor who lived in the same subdivision she did. Upon her return, mother witnessed to her also. It was a glorious visit. When I received word of her illness, I immediately packed and defiantly told Donald I was going to her. Shortly after I arrived, she died. To my great surprise, she had left my brothers and me an inheritance. A total of one hundred and fifty thousand dollars was to be divided between Johnny, Vaughn, and me. She had left her natural son only one dollar. We felt so bad for Tony that we gave him her home and the furnishings it contained, totally against the attorney's direction and Mother's wishes, but we had been rejected so much by our parents that our hearts were broken for him.

As soon as Donald realized that I was going to have money, his first words to me were, "I don't want this to change our life."

I said with a chuckle, *"You might not, but I do!"*

He gave me an ultimatum—either the money was going into a business or into the house. I told him if I had to choose, it would be the house because I wanted my children to know they always had a home. He readily agreed. But I was a little smarter, I thought. I told him if I was giving all of my money to him for the house, I wanted my name on the deed.

His response was, "No problem." He was going to buy the home place where we lived once he got through with the bankruptcy release, he said. The family went ahead and deeded the home to him, and he told me that he was going to his attorney to have them add my name. For some reason, I was not surprised when the deed arrived and my name wasn't on it. He had possession of all my money, and I never saw a dime of it, except for the little interest I drew out, which cost me a very frightening situation.

I went with him to the bank to open a new account for my money "to be used as needed in the renovation of the house." (I later learned that he had deposited only twenty-five thousand dollars. I do not know what happened to the other half of my inheritance.) The lady and I struck up a conversation, and before Donald was through with the transaction, it was like she and I had known each other forever. After I realized he had reneged on our agreement, I was upset that he had my money and I had nothing for it. I called the lady at the bank and asked her how much interest had accrued on the account. She told me there was eighteen hundred dollars, so I asked her to send it. To my surprise, she didn't hesitate. Two days later when I received the check, I bought curtains and bedspreads for the children and our bed. I bought rugs for the bathrooms and some new towels. Micah got new clothes and the new shoes I had promised him. The children also got clothes and shoes. I thought I was rich! I knew in my heart there would come a day of reckoning, but for the moment it didn't matter. Everyone had a smile on their faces and I loved it.

The day came; the call came all the way from Virginia.

Words of profanity came rolling out of his mouth as he yelled "What have you done with *my* money?"

"Well," I explained, "the amount in that account was only half the amount I received from my mother, so I thought it was fair to use the interest."

"You have exactly twenty-four hours to return it," he yelled, and then he hung up. Calculating the distance from where he was to where I was, I realized that I had approximately one hour. Within that hour, I packed our van full of clothes and then crowded in the four children. Micah was visiting his sister. I knew if I stayed, my life was in danger.

I went straight to a safe haven for families located behind my church. I went to the church as soon as I got the children settled in. I told my pastor what I had done. He smiled and told me I hadn't done anything wrong. He called Donald to tell him he needed to talk with him. Donald seemed less than interested, but eventually he showed up. My pastor asked Donald to tell his version of the story. Donald said he was actually holding that money for me for security. When asked what he thought I did wrong in spending the money, he said I spent it foolishly. The pastor asked him if I had curtains in the house before I bought the ones with that money, to which he answered, "No."

"How long have you lived there?"

"Two years." Then he asked about every other item I bought. The pastor told Donald that a woman had the desire to make a house a home, and what I did was not wrong, nor was it selfish. Everything I did was for the home or for someone else. The pastor then asked him how much he contributed to the family financially, to which he sat and stared, knowing I was sitting there and could say anything but the truth.

He finally said, "I guess nothing."

The pastor, already knowing the truth, said, "The family deserves more than that. If you want this marriage to work, you need to do this. Open an account in her name for the household. Put one thousand dollars in the account to start off with, and then put the same amount in each month. You've told me how much you have, and you can afford that."

Donald agreed to do as asked. The children and I went home.

For two months I had money to provide for my family. Then my checks started bouncing. I couldn't understand. When I checked the bank, I learned that he had made the deposits as promised, but every day he would withdraw money until everything he put in the account was gone. Finally, he just stopped making deposits.

Nothing had or would ever change with him. Again I was counting pennies to pay the electric and cable bills and buy groceries. (Donald had cable installed, but I had to pay the bills). I scrimped while he continued to spend his days walking the shopping mall, eating steak lunches, and driving his fine vehicles. He came home often with new clothes, shoes, boots, hats, and whatever he chose. We would watch him walk through the house with his purchases while the rest of us were in need. I confronted him about how it made everyone feel, to which he responded, "I knew you were jealous. Listen to yourself! Don't you sound silly. It's my money, and I will spend my money my way!"

I challenged him, "I thought you said God gave you your money. I believe if He did, He meant for you to share."

He ignored me.

When the two oldest girls were about nine and ten, a lady at church, which was Alice McDaniel, the same woman who had made an impact on me regarding a boss whose mouth yielded foul language, was crocheting multicolored collars for young girls. She was selling them for seven dollars each. All the girls wanted them, including my girls, who just smiled because they knew they couldn't get one. I remembered I had about forty-five dollars for grocery money, so I gave the lady fourteen dollars to give my girls something beautiful. They put them right on and wore them proudly. On the way home, Donald asked where they got them, and I told him. He began yelling and screaming because I bought them, telling me I didn't know how to spend money. I casually retorted that he was probably right. The only way you learn is by having something to learn with, and since I never had any money, I guessed I'd never learn!

For quite some time he had been carrying a very small pistol in his pocket, which didn't just alarm me, it terrified me. When I inquired about it, he would say things like, "You never know who you might meet in the men's room." His answer didn't make much sense to me, but I just accepted it.

Shortly after I confronted him about the gun, he had a confrontation with my brother, Vaughn, who had been guarding an auto glass repair business of Donald's. Vaughn was to be paid an agreed amount but had not been paid for quite some time. Vaughn asked for his money, and apparently it offended Donald. Before I knew it, Donald pulled the small pistol out of his pocket, and without thinking I stepped between Vaughn and the gun. I was carrying Synthia, but this made no difference to Donald. He continued to point the gun, threatening my life if I didn't get out of the way. He finally calmed down and the situation passed.

When it was over, I went home with Donald. It took me days to be able to talk with him again. At that point, I felt I despised him. He continued to threaten to use the gun. I listened to threats regarding others, to statements that the world would be a better place without him or her or them. I felt daily I was trying to save lives. I'd tell him he wasn't God, that God decides when it was someone's time to die, not him. He said that God uses people to make things happen. He really believed he was a "chosen one," and whatever he did was inspired by God.

From that time on, I never slept without the fear that each night could be the last night of my life. I was still walking close to God, reading the Bible most of the day, praying all of the time. It was all that sustained me, along with the gift of my children. But I lived in fear twenty-four hours every day, seven days a week.

Brandon, Heather, and Holly were all in high school. Brandon was playing football, but he hated school. I spent a lot of my time chasing him down to make sure he was in school everyday; he enjoyed other things outside of school because school was boring. For a while, I'd call every day just to be sure he was there.

Heather and Holly were cheerleaders and were always in the homecoming court. Heather won Homecoming Queen her senior year and was selected "Most Beautiful" of the Senior Superlatives. She won the principal's scholarship for college. Holly had other plans for her future for which the school she attended did not offer classes, so she opted to go to another local high school her senior year. She attended and graduated from Greeneville High School. She, too, was elected to the Homecoming Court. Brandon went to school and worked after school although still not fond of those confining walls. Synthia was cheerleading in her school and enjoyed sports, and she was also a Homecoming Participant. Above all though, she enjoyed her friends.

Although life outside the home for all of us was good, life at home was as bad as it could get. Then something worse happened. Brandon told me he wanted to live with his dad. It devastated me. My world was crumbling. He told me it wasn't anything I was doing wrong. He just needed his dad. I tried to understand, but it still hurt. It hurt so bad that I had to pray all the time, and when I wasn't praying, I was crying. Brandon called me daily long distance, until his dad got the phone bill. He convinced me that he loved me and there was nothing I did wrong, but I knew it was all about Donald, my choice had hurt my children when I thought I was making the best choice for my children. Brandon always assured me he just wanted to spend some of his teen age years close to his dad.

As the days went on, I still cried. One day as I prayed, "Send me some help. I need someone to help me through this." I saw a face in my mind, a face I hadn't seen in years. God is so good. He was preparing me for a phone call I would get proving He was in control. The next afternoon my phone rang. As soon as I answered and heard the voice, the face flashed in front of my eyes again. God *was* there in my prayers. I began saying, "Oh my goodness, oh my goodness," and I started to cry. It was Heidi, a sweet, beautiful woman of God. She said as she prayed that day, she had been led to call me. I shared with Heidi all that was going on regarding Brandon and my life with Donald. She listened, counseled, and prayed with me. She promised to continue to pray. I was so thankful because I knew beyond a shadow of a doubt that God had once again intervened in my confusion and pain. That certainly was not the last time.

Angels do exist, and God allows them to visit us, if only for a moment in time. But those are times you never, ever forget.

A few days after the phone call, I was still grieving but coping, with God's help. I continued to pray, and prayer brought me a sense of peace. Then I experienced a divine visitation. For reasons since forgotten, I was sitting at the mall with Donald in the open food court. I had just introduced myself to a lady sitting near me, and we began to converse. Donald was sitting at another table talking politics with some of his friends. All of a sudden, I realized that right in front of me the crowd seemed to part in a strange manner. As it did, an elderly gentleman with a cane proceeded toward me. He was looking straight at me, and I could not take my eyes off of him. There was nothing special to look at, but I was drawn. As he approached, he continued to hold my attention.

The old gentleman stopped in front of me, and he slowly but steadily lifted his cane and pointed it at me. "You need not worry," he said. "It will be all right. Things as they are now are not how they will always be. You must not be afraid, for you will live to see your nineties and when you die, you will die with a smile on your face. You are as beautiful on the inside as you are on the outside."

With that he lowered his cane and left the same way he came. As I sat trying to comprehend what had just happened, Donald jumped up from his seat and tried to follow him. Moments later, Donald came back, a little pale, and said the old man had vanished. He was nowhere to be seen.

The woman sitting beside me said, "Lonely old guy, wasn't he?"

I just grinned, but I was still in awe. Something very strange but beautiful had happened.

I sat quietly as Donald and I drove home, going over and over in my mind what had happened and the words that had been spoken. Donald confessed he thought I had been visited by an angel. I was still in awe, first that Donald had shared the experience, and that he believed as I did, it was an angel. Second because I believed God loved me so much, He saw the degree of my anguish and consoled me just as a father would. I must say even though Donald heard the exact words spoken, he did not like the newfound safety I had in those very words. He again tried to steal my security…he responded in anger towards me for standing my ground which was against his will and said, "Maybe God really was telling you that you will live to see your 1990s!" implying that if I didn't do what he said, my 1990s might be all I would see alive. For a space of time, his words, along with my lack of trust in God's Words, threw me back into the unsecured world where I had been before. The Holy

Spirit continued to beckon me and minister to me, and I became strong again and rebuked the words of Donald. God, in his loving message through the words of the angel, was assuring me of safety, long life, and Brandon was coming home. I have never doubted any of that since. Donald could not harm me because God was in control. I went over and over everything in my mind. Why did God choose to send an angel in the form of an old man? I came to the conclusion that a child might be too unbelievable, a woman just wouldn't have made the same impression on me, and a young man would have probably sent Donald into a jealous rage, but an old man represented wisdom, strength, and respect. God knew what messenger to send.

It took five months, but Brandon did come back home. I knew he would. He was different, and we had major issues. He lacked respect and discipline. He was an angry child. I had dealt with these problems before by myself, but now I had help. I would even be awakened at night with the urge to pray. "Pray! Pray right this minute!" As I began to pray, I always looked at the clock on the wall in front of my bed. Often, I would say to Brandon, "Son, I don't know why, but God awakened me to pray at two o'clock this morning. I know it was for you." He wouldn't say anything for days, but then he'd tell me how at that very time on that very night he was about to become involved in some activity that would get him in trouble—such as a fight—and he somehow managed to stay away from such involvement. He also felt the love and protection God had for him.

What was really peculiar about my relationship with my children was that they could be anywhere in the world and do something wrong and I'd know about it by the time they got home. Brandon's friends accused me of having a tracking device inserted into his body at birth. Heather was usually level-headed and did what was expected of her. If I told her to be home at eleven o'clock, she'd be home at ten thirty. However, her temper sometimes got her in trouble. The door to her room would often slam when things upset her. Then there was fun-loving Holly. If I told her to be home by eleven, I'd get a call at ten minutes before her deadline. "I'm on my way. I was watching a movie and the time got away."

Then there was Brandon. "Don't make me a girl," he'd complain when I gave him a curfew of eleven o'clock. He was home by eleven o'clock—the next morning! "I'm a boy. I need to take the girl home first," was his argument. His curfew became such an issue that he moved in with some friends. I accepted his decision this time, but I knew his life had taken a wrong turn. I prayed continuously for his protection, as I did for all my children. Eventually, he moved back home. A child had left my home, and a responsible man returned.

In the meantime, Donald's business failed and he blamed his partners. One of the partners, a well-known businessman from Mosheim, came to our home to talk with Donald. I knew as soon as I saw Donald's hand slide into his pocket that trouble was stirring. I grabbed his arm as he started out the front door. He looked at me and yanked away, his facial expressions would have scared the devil himself.

"Please don't do this. Think of your child and how she will have to live the rest of her life," I begged.

"Her life and everyone else's will be better off without that man around," he yelled back as he went flying out the door.

"Let God make that decision," I said, hanging onto the door.

"He already has." All I knew to do was pray. I gave it to God. Shortly, he came back inside and the visitor drove away. He said he threatened him with the gun when the man got irate with him. I didn't want to discuss it anymore. We didn't need to. God was in control.

Sweet Micah was always stirring around. From time to time, I'd take him to town. He'd get all dressed up. It was special just to get to go to town. One day as we drove to town, I looked at him in the rearview mirror and said, "Micah, is there anywhere you would like to go?"

He hesitated a minute, rubbed his chin, and said, "Well, the other day when I was watching television, I saw Disney World. I think I'd like to see that!"

I had no idea he'd pick somewhere like that. I was thinking

perhaps the park, or Gatlinburg, maybe even a trip to the lake. Disney World was a twelve-hour drive away. I thought maybe he'd forget about that "want," but I couldn't. Every time I would look at him, I'd think: *This sixty-four-year-old man has been to town an average of three times a year. No one ever takes him anywhere. The woods and the creek on the farm are all he's seen in his life, except when he goes to church.*

That day I made a decision. Whatever it took, I would see that Micah got his wish. I started working on it and learned that if I got a group of people to go, we could go at reduced rates or even free if the group was sufficiently large. Knowing Donald was fonder of his money than he was of us, I began recruiting a group. Eventually, I had fifty-eight people committed. I chartered the bus, rented condos one mile outside the gate at Disney World, bought tickets in advance, and off we went. The trip was long and hard, but fun. Micah was in awe of all the sights. He got to see the ocean, highways, tall buildings, and ride a bus. Once at Disney World, I got everyone in line and passed out the entry tickets. Suddenly, I realized Micah was not in the line. My heart raced. Micah had a hard time seeing at times, and I knew the crowds could disorient him. I quickly sent Heather, Holly, and Brandon in search of him. Then I recalled telling him if for some reason he got lost to find the parking lot and get on our bus. I ran all the way to the bus, opened the door, and saw a familiar hat about half-way down the isle.

"Micah," I said, "where have you been? We've been looking everywhere for you."

He replied, "Well, you told me if I got lost to come back to the bus."

I said, "Yes, I did and you did well, but where did we lose you?"

"Right over there," he said, pointing at the entrance booths. *Poor Micah*, I thought, *he didn't even get in the gate.*

"Are you ready to go in now?" I asked him.

"No, I'll just sit right here."

"But, Micah, we came all this way for you to see Disney World."

"And I seen it," he responded. "Don't have to go in it. I just wanted to see it." He spent the remainder of the time in the condo, picking oranges off the trees and watching television. He was happy. He was special!

There was another event that proves that, given the time and attention, persons with learning disabilities such as Micah could work towards educating. A family reunion was coming up, and Micah was excited, except for the fact that everyone signed a guest book showing who had attended. Everyone signed their own name. Micah wanted to sign his, but all he could do was spell it aloud. He had no idea how to write. Every night for weeks and weeks, after supper we sat down and practiced, and eventually he learned how to spell his name legibly. He was so proud. I was so proud, but not as much as when he walked through the doors of the reception hall. He walked that "Micah walk" over to the podium, picked up the pen, and wrote his name. I felt like I had just birthed a baby again. Everyone was running over to the podium, looking at what Micah had written, he stood grinning. As I stood there watching as he grinned, I could see he was swelling with pride. I also swelled with pride.

Shortly, Donald had another business go under because, he said, the office manager he'd employed for many, many years had been embezzling. He used me day and night working with accountants to find out exactly how much she took. During this time, my family had to fend for themselves. The girls cared for Synthia, being a mother to her in my absence. While working late one evening, I got a call from the girls. They were sobbing. I could barely understand what was wrong. As I calmed them down, I learned that Micah was the target of a driver playing "chicken" and was hit and left in a ditch for hours. Micah had walked to a nearby church and was walking home. He was unable to move due to his injuries, and no one knew how long he had lain there unconscious. The lights of a passing car helped the driver to see him. The driver stopped and then came to the house to call 911—Micah was rushed by ambulance, to the Johnson City Medical Center.

For six long weeks, Micah was in a coma. I stayed with him day and night, only going home long enough to see my children, bathe, and change clothes. I brought him a tape player and earphones. At home we recorded the family talking to him and his favorite church music. Hospital staff told us they could tell a difference in his blood pressure and vital signs when he was listening to the tapes. He never got to come home. He could never walk again. He spent his remaining years in a nursing home and died in 1998, several years after the accident. I will forever be grateful a way was made available to take him to Disney World, even if he was satisfied just to see it.

When I realized Micah would not be able to return home, I went in search of a job. I found a job with the local newspaper. Donald never wanted me to work, but seeing that his child needed more than he wanted to pay for and now Micah's Social Security check was no longer available, he agreed. It was the beginning of the end. I was under so much stress that I could not concentrate on my job. Daily I was concerned about bills, children, the defective car I used for transportation, and a husband who didn't care. I worried about who would pick up Synthia after school and who would stay with her. Donald could have done all of these things to help out, but he chose to spend his days at the mall. The girls did their best to help, but they both were working two jobs.

One time when I was so short of money (usually in winter, when electric bills were higher), I sneaked into his closet before he got up and got two dollars out of his wallet for Synthia's lunch. The next morning I did the same thing—not a dime more. The third morning I opened his wallet and a piece of paper fell out. On it was written "two tens, three fives, and five ones." He was letting me know he'd caught me. He began locking the closet door because he believed people were stealing his clothes.

The weather had turned extremely cold, so one evening I turned the heat on so the children's rooms would be warm. Later that night, the girls came to my room to say they were freezing. I went downstairs and checked the thermostat and realized it had been turned off. I shook my head in disbelief and started to doubt that I had actually turned it on. I turned it to seventy degrees, and went back upstairs. In the morning when I went down to get the children up for school, their rooms were freezing. I immediately went over to the thermostat, thinking something was wrong with it. It was turned down to fifty degrees. Infuriated, I turned it back up and ran up the steps to confront Donald. His response to my anger was if I thought they could pay the power bill, they could use it. I reminded him that any bills were paid by Micah and the children, and now Micah's check was no longer coming. He sarcastically replied, "Two hundred dollars a month! You act like that's so much." I responded angrily, "When it's all you've got, it's everything!"

We had two heating units in the house—one for our room upstairs and one for downstairs. Of course, the upstairs was always warm.

I felt like a terrible mother. I didn't know what to do. After pleading and begging him not to let the children be cold, he bought a ceramic heater to heat their bedrooms and the bathroom. It helped, but it was still very cold. The remainder of the downstairs had no heat. Finally, I decided to tell the children to turn up the heat after they heard us go to bed. Donald heard the heat pump come on. He grabbed a hammer and angrily ran downstairs. I followed him. After repeated blows to the thermostat, he knocked it off the wall. He then turned, looked at me, and said, "Well, that takes care of that situation." He brushed by me and went back to bed. I went to the children's rooms and tearfully apologized.

It was at this point I realized our marriage didn't have a chance of lasting. Amidst my tears, I prayed, "Dear God, I've always prayed for you to help me feel love for Donald. This time I ask you to keep it. I don't want it. I'm tired of hurting, tired of the children hurting. Please do not let me love Donald...ever!"

Food was all I enjoyed besides my children and my church. I gained about fifty-five pounds eating the cheapest thing that could be fixed—biscuits and gravy. When I began working, even with the additional weight, men at work gave me compliments. They made me feel better about myself. I hadn't had much attention in my whole life except for High School and the wrong kind here and there. I began to look forward to these men coming by my desk. I actually craved the attention.

As time progressed, I began comparing the way they treated me to the way Donald treated me. It gave me the desire to look better, therefore I felt better. All those "other men" were actually making me smile. I knew this was wrong, but after spending more than almost two decades feeling nothing but bad in my relationships, I felt justified. I was enjoying myself. After all, *I thought* it was innocent. I put God out of my mind for a while and tried to enjoy what was happening to me. God never let me go.

One day while at work, Synthia called me from school crying. Her dad had taken her to school, and she had forgotten to take her lunch money. When she realized what she had done, she asked him for money for lunch.

He responded, "I have just enough for breakfast at McDonald's. If I give it to you, I won't be able to eat."

I talked to the school secretary and made arrangements for her to eat, and I promised to send the money the next day. I considered ending our marriage, but I didn't.

Another day I was at work and Synthia called. She'd forgotten to tell me about a five-dollar fee needed for her health class. If she didn't have the money that day, she would fail the class. Her dad had again taken her to school, and she asked him for the money. He told her, "I don't have five dollars."

She pleaded with him, "I promise I will pay you back.

"I'm going to be in so much trouble."

"Well, just how will you pay me back?" he asked.

"I have some money at home. I'll give it to you as soon as I get home."

"Okay," he agreed as he pulled a crisp five-dollar-bill out of his wallet. "But I expect payment back from you today." She agreed but cried later at school. She knew she didn't have five dollars at home. She called me and I told her, "Don't worry. This is not going to go on much longer." I knew our marriage was over.

The day I left our home, never to return, was a memorable day. Heather and Holly had both married, and Brandon was on his own. Synthia was celebrating her birthday, and four girls from church spent the night with her. The early morning hours brought a strong thunderstorm with tremendous winds. I heard the roof over the master bedroom rip off around five o'clock in the morning. By six o'clock Donald was up and dressed. As he walked out the door, he yelled back at me to call the contractor and have him come over and fix it, then call the insurance company. I told him I thought he should call since I had no idea where to start calling. He just looked at me and told me to do what he said, then drove off.

I tried to find a telephone number for the man who had remodeled the house, but I couldn't. The rain was falling so fast and hard I couldn't see across the lawn to the driveway. Soon rain was pouring into the house and through the base of the chandelier on the balcony. Lights started flickering, and I knew something bad was about to happen. I kept trying to get Donald on his cell phone, but he did not answer. By ten o'clock the rain was pouring in sheets through the door of Synthia's room, next to the master bedroom on the second floor. The girls thought this was an adventure and were bringing pots, pans, buckets, anything they could find to catch the water. Suddenly, water started pouring all across the doorframe of the master bedroom and the lights continued to flicker. There was nothing I could do. At one o'clock, I told the girls to gather their things and I'd take them home. I'd had enough. Donald had been gone for more than seven hours. He knew there was a problem and hadn't even called to check on us. As far as I was concerned, he could continue to do whatever he was doing. He had proven over and over again he didn't care. Synthia and I were out of there, forever, and it felt good.

About eleven o'clock that night I called him. He answered and asked where I was. I told him I was in Greeneville and we were staying in Greeneville. He didn't quite understand, so I detailed it for him.

He paused and said with a sigh, "You picked the worst time to leave me."

"Why?" I asked.

He said, "Because I think I'm going to have a heart attack."

I told him I would drive to get him and take him to the hospital, but he would have to meet me outside because I wasn't going in that house. He agreed to come outside when I arrived. I got

Synthia out of bed and made the twenty-five minute trip, praying all the way. I was truly hoping he would be okay. When I got there, he came outside and said he was feeling better, and then he asked if I would come in and talk with him. I told him, "Absolutely not! I never wanted to be back in that house again!" "What's the problem?" he asked, I was glad to fill him in.

"You have proven over and over how much you don't care instead of proving how much you care. What happened today was the final straw! While I hate what you've done, I do not hate you. I *will* take you to the hospital."

"I'm okay," he said, but he got in my car. I was a little concerned about his quick temper and the actions he might take, so I started driving towards Greeneville. He tried and tried to convince me to come back and try again.

"Not anymore!" I continually responded.

Finally, I turned around and took him back to his house, my heart pounding in fear. I made it quite obvious to him that I was not at all happy with the situation. He asked me as he got out of the car, "Can't you remember anything good about our marriage?"

I answered, "Synthia!"

He asked, "Is that all?"

I said, "There might have been more, but the bad ate it up."

"Was life with me that bad?" he asked.

I said, "Let's put it this way, living with you was like living with a king in a palace, seeing a large table set with everything that would satisfy your hungry body, but you knew you could only have the crumbs that fell to the ground *that couldn't* be swept up in a dust pan. That's what it was like living with you." With that, I drove off, feeling freedom as though I just had stepped out of a prison.

I filed for divorce. My friend Trudy sent me the money, I didn't ask her to, nor did she specify what it was for, but it was the exact amount of money needed, a gift, she said. I was so grateful. The "new me" became more direct, and I was not going to let him control me or my children's lives ever again. I often found myself angry often to the point of boiling whenever I'd hear his name or see him. However, as I became bolder, I also became weaker. I looked to myself for strength and often doubted that I could follow through with my intentions. I knew God was there, but I tried to ignore him, afraid of what He wanted me to do, like perhaps stay with Donald.

For eighteen years I had lived in a turbulent, wasteful prison in some aspects; however, the relationship I developed with God was truly a blessing; had I not experienced that life, I may never have realized how much I needed God.

I also realized that I couldn't blame anyone else for that life. I made a choice; no matter what excuses I had, I was still the one who made it. No one put me there. I chose the wrong partner and did some very wrong things. I truly deserved what I got, but the children didn't. God had been generous and merciful to me. Four wonderful things had resulted from that marriage. First, I developed a close walk with God because He sustained me. I turned away for a season, but He didn't leave me. Second, Synthia was a special gift. I would do it all again to be her mother. Although we have gone through some very turbulent times, she has blessed my life. Third, I learned how to raise a family of seven on nearly nothing and did not depend on public assistance. My children have learned how to be frugal. I could have applied for and received public assistance, except I lived with a millionaire! And fourth, Micah—what a blessing to have known him. He was special.

It took nearly a year to get to court in a state where you can get a divorce decree in three months. Donald kept putting it off, proposing one agreement after another. During all this time, he didn't support either of us. My job at the newspaper could not sustain us, so I took a second job. We managed financially, but I didn't spend the time that I should have with my young daughter. I grieve over that still because it was damaging to her.

One evening I got a call from Donald. He told me he was having some chest pains, although I knew he was a manipulator, and at that moment I suspected he was using some unethical means to gain some ground, I still didn't want to take a chance, so I gave him the benefit of the doubt. He needed to go to the hospital and didn't want to drive himself. Synthia and I drove him to the hospital in Johnson City. The cardiologist at the hospital diagnosed a triple blockage. He went through surgery, and we stayed at the hospital with him. When it was all over and time for him to go home, he told me the doctor said he couldn't go home alone and he could not climb the stairs to his bedroom. I consented to let him stay at our place for a few days to recuperate. He slept in my bed, while Synthia and I slept in hers. He made all sorts of excuses not to go home, and I began to be concerned that he was getting too comfortable and was not going to leave. I called his oldest daughter and asked if she could take him home with her. She agreed. While I was at work the following day, she came and took him to her home.

I wasn't sensitive to how all of this was affecting Synthia until I found a note she had written, stating she was too much trouble, she cost too much, she wished she had never lived, and that she often contemplated death. She also talked about her relationship with her dad and how she had negative feelings about their relationship. She also stated how angry she was he had come to stay with us. I realized at that moment that my child was having some dangerously negative thoughts; although justified, it still alarmed me and showed a key sign she was unhealthy. Although I didn't want to share a life with Donald, I didn't hate him, nor did I wish anything ill towards him. At times, I felt hate but later realized that it was what he was doing that I hated. I found Synthia some help where she was able to vent her feelings and heal. She learned to deal with her emotions concering her dad. The ball was in his court.

A newspaper office is a public place, and people come and go at will. Donald would come in and hang around the office often never really bothering me, but letting me know he was on the premises. I couldn't give my full attention to my job for fear of how he might embarrass me or what he might tell my co-workers. With that, as well as the unhealthy relationships I had allowed myself to become a part of, certainly stifled my healthy growth as a Christian, as well as my Christian witness. As the Holy Spirit made that realization clear to me, I turned in my notice to Mary Agnes, my friend and boss. She had so often encouraged me, counseled me, and was a wonderful example of a Christian. I gave a two weeks' notice without a totally truthful explanation. I'm sure everyone knew, but I was too ashamed to admit.

# CHAPTER TEN

The divorce was final! I cannot tell you the degree of happiness I felt. It was like I had just walked out of a dark dungeon where I had been held captive for a century. I dated several men but was not going to commit myself to any of them. I made a few of them angry and, in retrospect, I probably used their company to fill my loneliness. My full intentions were to remain single for the rest of my life. I spent a season of time outside of God's will and again found myself in relationships that were unhealthy especially, as I mentioned before, for my Christian growth. However, after two years of ignoring God's charge in my life, I found all I wanted now was to devote my life to God, family, and friends. I was fine with that. That was safe. That was right, and I wanted right.

In retrospect, I see by God allowing me to be on my own, which I had never been before, brought me to the realization that I cannot live a fulfilled life apart from him…what a mess I had made.

I got a new job in the Human Resource department with the help of a gentleman from church named Vann, who, by the way, was the husband of Debbie, daughter of Helen Rollins (Sorrells). My new job was with Forwardair/Landair Transport Company, owned by a kind man who shares his blessings with our town. I made great friends there, and many of them remain friends. Donald couldn't get to me there; it was safe. I loved my job and the people I worked with. They respected me.

I bought a condominium for Synthia and myself. What a joy I felt to be in *my* own home. No one could take it away unless I quit making payments. I thank Janice Bradley and Bill Hickerson from a local bank, without whom my first real home would not have been possible. They will always be special to me. They did something no one else ever did for me: they gave me a home, my home. I loved the idea of being in control of my life with God in the pilot's seat. No more trying to please a self-centered husband who thought of no one but himself.

I bought a car, one that stopped at stop signs and started with a key. I was ecstatic. This, too, came as a blessing that Janice and Bill from that same local bank approved. I was in a place I had never experienced before; my very own secure space. I asked God's forgiveness for ignoring him and for the years I allowed myself to be consumed in my earthly desires. I truly missed my relationship with him. I really missed talking to him and hearing his voice. I prayed for forgiveness, he heard me and forgave me. How loving is that after all I had done?

I began teaching Sunday school for high school girls and loved it. I wasn't just teaching. I was learning from them too. I was strong and at the best place I had been in years. I was right where I wanted to be, growing closer to God. God was using me.

God had another plan for me. I met Donna, a very attractive person who would become my friend. She loved to dance, especially the Shag. She heard there was a group meeting in Johnson City and asked me to take her. She had a kidney condition that eventually took her life. This same condition would cause her to become very ill from time to time, and she was afraid to travel alone. I had no idea what the Shag was, but on Monday nights I had nothing to do, so I drove her there. It was fun. I learned the basics but chose to sit and watch most of the time. Donna was a great dancer. We went back the next Monday and then the next, then something happened. That something changed my life. *It's good to be good to others! It always comes back to you.*

That Monday night in May 2000, I was sitting there in that dimly lit dance room, watching Donna, when a group of men entered the room. I glanced at them as they came in, one particular man caught my attention. He was the best-looking man I had ever seen. He wasn't very tall, had graying hair. He had a mustache and a dark tan. Despite his gray hair, he looked young. He glanced my way, and I quickly looked away. Then he came over and asked Donna to dance. Their dance was soon over, and he looked at me.

I tried hard to act like I didn't notice him, but he approached me anyways, asking, "Would you like to dance?"

When I hesitated, he asked, "Why not?"

I answered, "Because you really don't want to look like a fool, and with me you will. I don't know how to Shag."

He quickly responded, "I'll teach you," and with that he took my hand and led me to the dance floor. I floated. I could not feel the floor beneath my feet. Not since Ted had I felt those butterflies.

While we danced, he asked me where I was from and if I was single. Then he told me about his children and that he was a widower. He spoke lovingly of his wife who had died of cancer the year before at the age of forty-five. He told me how wonderful their marriage was; his eyes filled with tears as he remembered her. My heart was taken!

The next day we had lunch, and he looked even more handsome in the daylight. I was so proud to be seen with him. After several more dates with him, I realized I was surrendering the heart I had sworn never to give again. I couldn't wait to tell my children. The girls were excited for me, but Brandon was a little more cautious. "You'd better watch out," he warned. "He's a married man, Mom. No one acts like that. Have you ever been to his house?"

"Uh, no, I haven't," I answered.

"Case closed," he stated. "He dates women from towns other than where he lives. He's too good to be true, Mom." I realized he could be right.

The next time I talked with Jim, I was honest with him, and I told him what Brandon had said; after all, I had been ignorant too many times before, not again. He laughed. That night he took me to his home to meet his deceased wife's sister and her husband, who were staying in his house while their house was being built. They were such nice people. All my fears vanished.

About a month into the relationship, however, Jim shared with me his fears of another permanent relationship. It jolted me. I thought we were getting along well and was amazed he didn't seem to think the same. We were going to church together, we never had cross words, and we had fun. I just didn't understand.

Maybe I wasn't young or pretty enough. He was so handsome and so personable. Maybe I was too heavy. Maybe I wasn't sexy enough to keep his attention. Something was wrong, and I knew it was me.

The next day he called again and came over that night. He told me the reasons for his fears. He confessed to me that he had been seeing another woman before me, which was no surprise. What was surprising was she still called him and wasn't willing to let him go. He told me that they had agreed to date other people, but now she was calling him and making demands he honor a commitment he had made to her before he met me. He kindly agreed they would go on as friends as well as honor his commitment. He also said it was apparent it wasn't going to be easy to get her to release him, as she was calling constantly and showing up at his door. He asked if I would agree to wait until he could end this relationship with dignity. I just sat there. Then he said, "I know you'll be gone and be a part of someone else's life if I ask you to do that." I just continued to look at him. He surely felt no promises from me and finally promised to totally end his relationship with her after he honored his previous obligation to her.

He also added he was still grieving over his wife's death, and it was too soon to consider a permanent relationship. He felt that was where we were headed, and it scared him. His deceased wife was still *"the love of his life,"* and he thought it wasn't fair to go into a permanent relationship with those feelings still so apparent, and *that I could understand.* I at no time pressed him for a permanent stance; however, I also believed that was where we were headed.

That night my friend Wendy called and invited me to have dinner with her. She knew I was depressed, and we chose a restaurant where we had eaten before. We were seated next to a window. As we waited for our food, Jim drove into the parking lot with his date. My heart stopped. Of all the places in two counties, he chose the same restaurant! I wanted to leave, but Wendy said, "You're not going anywhere!"

"Oh, yes, I am," I said, and I stood to leave. I didn't look at him as I left, although I had to pass him. He had gotten out of his car saw me and jumped back in his car. I suppose he thought there was going to be a confrontation.

Sick at heart, I just wanted to go home. I shouldn't have been jealous. He had told me the truth, but I just didn't want to see it.

I got home about nine o'clock, at ten-thirty my phone rang. The Caller ID feature on my phone showed the number I recognized was his. I almost chose not to answer it, but I did. The first words were mine. "I'm sorry. I would never have gone there if I knew you would be there."

He said he knew that, but after he saw me, he questioned himself about what he was doing with the wrong person. It healed the hurt. I told him he was wonderful, and I had enjoyed his company. If God was in control of this relationship, I told him, then I had to accept the outcome. I told him I had always made the choices before not allowing God to be the ultimate deciding factor.

I told him I would always remember him in the best of ways, and although he was the most wonderful man I had ever known, if it wasn't right for him, then it wasn't right at all, but more than that, if it wasn't God's choice then it definitely wasn't right for either of us. I thanked him and promised that if we ever ran into each other again, I would be friendly. He became very quiet, and we hung up.

The following day I received an e-mail from him. I still have it to this day. He told me, over the years women had demanded his affections, but he'd never had one willing just to let him go without a struggle. He said that made a difference. He got to choose and not be chosen. Because of that, I have been blessed that he chose me.

I had an astonishing revelation, *I had finally let go of the fears*, the fears of being alone that forever followed me. The fear that Satan had held over me was gone. I actually relied on the only one who is reliable, and that's my Holy Father. When I willingly let go of Jim, it allowed God to act. The holy, wonderful life He had waiting for me finally was no longer a dream. It had become reality!

From that day Jim and I were together as much as we could. Our hearts grew together and, because of his honesty and my willingness to let him go, it made our relationship stronger. Whenever we had differences, we worked them out. It was the relationship I had always wanted but began to believe would not happen to me. I kept waiting for something to go wrong. Six years later, it still hasn't. My children love him and the grandchildren adore him. He is genuine. I believe with all my heart that God's hand was in our meeting and falling in love.

On March 17, 2001, Jim Sexton and I were married at his home on Douglas Lake in Dandridge, Tennessee. My foster dad, Reverend Charles Hutchins, officiated. Mom Hutchins was there, too, looking as beautiful as always. It was so special. Our friends and family were there to share in the excitement of the event.

I'll never forget what Brandon said to me that day: "Mom, you have finally found someone to love and take care of you."

Jim continues to care for my every need and much, much more. Not only is he good to me, but he is always there for all of the children and grandchildren in our blended families. He is the most unselfish, giving person I've ever known. I am so blessed.

He has told me so many times that he actually prayed to God to send someone like me, and, because he knows that God answered that prayer, his whole life is devoted to making me happy. I certainly would not want to live my life again, but I would go through it all to know it would turn out this way. If I were to die today, I would die a happy woman. I am living the life I believed was only possible in dreams, the life that a social worker once told me was only a fantasy.

With our marriage came Jim's wonderful sister, Faye, and her very loving family, including her husband, Hubert, and sons, Chris and Matt. Matt is married to Leann. Matt and Leann are parents of twins: Hannah, who is into every aspect of being a *girlie* girl, while Kyle is an outdoor sportsman. Jim's brother Delmar and his wife, Phyllis, have become a brother and sister to me. We've enjoyed countless hours of family time together, including vacations and just hanging-out. They are the prime examples of what Christians should be. My grandchildren adore them. Jim's youngest brother is Daniel. He is a guy who loves life. He finds more to do than anyone I know and usually gets the rest of us involved. The past few years, he and his precious wife, Linda, have had us involved in selling Nascar programs and merchandise at several of the Nascar races. I have never worked so hard in all my life. He wears us out! We love them.

Heather and Holly are godly mothers and wives. Watching their lives makes me think that something I did was right, if nothing more than to point them to Jesus. They married identical twin brothers, Mike and Roger Davis, who are the best of the best. They can do anything! All we have to do is say, "We're going to do this," or, "We are going to build that." When we start, they show up whether we ask them to or not. They don't stop until it's done, and when it's done, it's near perfect. Heather and Mike have three children: Logan, Dylan, and Isabella and again not to forget Tanner, along with others lost. Holly and Roger also have three children: Alexis, Noah, and Victoria. Brandon married Jama Whitson, the best daughter-in-law in the world. She is beautiful inside and out. Brandon is a son any mother would be proud of; he's a very hard worker and gives everything he does one hundred percent. I am so blessed. Brandon and Jama, have a daughter, Megan—she is just as beautiful as her momma and one of my little chic-a-dees. Synthia remains single, but she has plenty of time to marry and start a family. She is beautiful. Although I know she has had many hurdles in her life, just as my life, she will, with the help of God, cross them all with victory. Our children have embraced each other as siblings, Jamie, Nikisha, and Angie, I adore them. We often get together to share family times. Jim has accepted and has been accepted by my brothers, with whom I am still very close. My nephew, Tad, also respects him to the nth degree. My family is complete, and no one can take that from me. We are a blessed family.

My brother Johnny is a godly man, and he and his son, Tad, are extremely close. My brother Vaughn, who is also a professing Christian, is single and has a dog he claims as his son. Vaughn would be a great stand-up comedian but, unfortunately, he lives with narcolepsy, a sleeping disorder caused by a chemical imbalance in his brain. He handles it well and readily jokes about it. After living several years in Greeneville, he has settled in Asheville, North Carolina along with Johnny and Tad.

Mom and Dad Hutchins, who have been instrumental in areas of healing for me, have returned to Greeneville after many years in South Carolina. I often see Camille, Ralph, and John and their families when they visit. We're all back together.

I reflect on where I came from and where I am now, and I truly thank God for His patience, generosity, and loving hand helping to guide me to the "Blessed Road" he had waiting for me while I bumped around in those dark years, unable to find it. I am so thankful for the unconditional love of my husband, which has inspired me to look the best I can. I have lost almost all the weight I had gained over those horrible years. But not before Jim married me *with* the weight, which added to the healing because he loved me even when I wasn't my best. He told me he saw something special inside of me, and that's what he fell in love with. He deserves the best I can be. I'm not there yet, but I'm on my way.

I sit and wonder if I had met Jim first and lived a normal life, would I have appreciated him? Would I realize how fortunate and blessed I am? Would we be as happy? Would I take who or what he is for granted? I hope not.

Just as I think the same about God, if I had always known about him in the way I do now, would I appreciate who he is and what he means! I'm just glad I see what a blessing both those relationships are—blessings from God.

Over the years I have learned some very hard lessons, some gentle lessons, but for certain all growing lessons. During the years I spent in adult rebellion, I truly believe God lovingly stepped aside long enough for me to live for the very first time under my own control with absolutely no one telling me what to do. I had never had that freedom. During that time, it became obvious that I could not control my life in a healthy state. I needed to learn that, for I would have never realized it if I had not experienced it. Without Him, life is empty.

When I began writing my story, I could not look at the words on the page. I typed with my eyes shut tightly. There was too much pain to revisit. Only later, when I *had* to review my manuscript, did I actually read what I had written. Somehow, as I read what I had for so long hidden, I found peace. It was apparent;

God's spirit carried me most of my life. This experience of sharing has been very therapeutic for me, especially in the sense of my spirituality.

My grandchildren love coming to our home. Finally I have the home I never had and the love I never experienced. The "fantasy" has become reality. I heard the grandchildren talking amongst themselves several years ago, discussing "The Happy House." Unsure of where that was, I asked them. They looked up at me with the eyes of innocence and truth. Their response made my eyes well up in tears. "It's your house, Nana!" How I thank God for my "Happy House" and for the happy family He has given me.

I want the words "See you at the Happy House" inscribed on my gravestone when I die; after all, that is the ultimate Happy House.

I pray often "Thank you, loving God, for my Happy House here on earth, and thank you for the one you are preparing for me in heaven. Both have been worth waiting for!"

"Little Girl Sittin"

Little girl sittin'
by the side of the road

kickin' up dust
with her dirty little toes

Nobody wants her
though she doesn't know why,
existing in the shadows of everybody's life.

Her momma has left her,
her daddy's down on luck,
this little girl's afraid, but
she hasn't given up

She cries, "Nobody wants me, I don't know why,"
then she leans back her head towards the big blue sky.

I don't know what's up there,
but I feel it's something's good,
I'd like to fly and take a peek if only I could.

She still misses Momma and wonders where she's at,
while everyday she wanders down that well-beaten
path.
She stares down the road where she's been sittin' at,
and patiently she watches 'cause her momma's
comin' back.

Little girl sittin'
by the side of the road,
in a dirty cotton dress,
with a dirty little nose.

Many years have come
and many years have gone,
now this little girl has a girl of her own.

Everyday she's thankful
for now she understands,
for when no one else was caring,
there was a "Special Hand."
A mother and a father all rolled into one,
God our Heavenly Father—Jesus Christ his Son.

In a pretty cotton dress,
with shiny matching shoes,
with a clean little face,
things her mother never knew.

Nobody wanted her, though she never knew why.
But no longer does she wonder about the big blue sky,
God's loving hand each night tucked her into bed,
kissed her on the cheek, and made sure she was fed.

Little girl sittin' on her momma's lap,
made up for the loneliness,
Momma felt from the past.

When asked if she wished for a life without such pain,
she held her daughter closer and carefully began.
"Years have come, and years have gone,
and I still don't understand,"
although it was quite painful, I'm now certain of whose I am."
If I were offered a very different life,
I would not change a thing,
to be where I am today was worth everything.

*written by Rita Sexton*

# EPILOGUE

In conclusion, I should not forget that my biological dad eventually gave his heart to Jesus. He made his commitment to Jesus some ten years before he died. Even before he realized he was dying, he spent the rest of his life witnessing to people. My dad had worked for the City of Johnson City, Tennessee, for many years. When he retired, he was given a retirement party by the City and was covered by the local news. He had become a man of respect. The ole' sinner man died long before my dad took his last breath. He spent his last days as a "bag boy" at the local Food City, near his home, because he knew he could reach the most people for Christ there. I was proud to stand at his casket and claim he was my dad. He died in 2001.

Our adoptive mother also gave her heart to Jesus many, many years after the painful experience of the dessert dipped in alcohol. We stayed close, because I treasured the good things she had taught me, and I respected the fact that she at least taught me to be a lady. I never forgot her at Christmas, Mother's Day, or her birthday. I forgave her as I did my biological dad. She died in 1987.

My biological mother comes in and out of our lives, which is typical. I have forgiven her; however, her lifestyle is still one that I choose not to share. She visits one week, and it takes me a month to get over it, literally, but the act of forgiveness is cleansing for me. I look at it this way: at least she gave us life.

I have spoken with her often of how Jesus will transform a person's life; apparently, she doesn't see the need...yet.

I recall the last words that Donald spoke to me several years ago. In his usual controlling way, he said, "I know one thing for certain, I got the best years of your life!" At first it upset me, but as I thought about it a moment, I realized he got some years, yes, *but certainly not the best.*

As far as my adoptive dad, I have forgiven him, although we do not have a relationship at all other than an occasional talk on the phone. I try to not bear any negative emotions. My brothers, on the other hand, do have a relationship with him, which is great for them; after all, he was one of the greatest dads ever...until it changed for me.

Ted has remarried to a wonderful Christian woman, who is highly respected by Heather, Holly, Brandon, and me.

Donald, who has not remarried, remains in contact with Synthia. They have a caring relationship.

# ABOUT THE AUTHOR

Author Rita Sexton lives with her husband Jim in Dandridge, Tennessee, about a forty-five-minute-drive from the town she owes so much, Greeneville, Tennessee. Her daughters, Heather, Holly, and Synthia also live in Greeneville. Brandon, his wife, Jama, and daughter, Megan, have recently moved to New Bern, North Carolina, where Brandon has transferred with a new company. Jamie and his family live about thirty minutes from Greeneville, in Johnson City, Tennessee. Angie lives in Kingsport, just minutes away as well.

Rita and Jim attend Towering Oaks Baptist Church in Greeneville, along with Heather and family, Holly and family, Synthia, and until recently Brandon and family. Both Jim and Rita have been active in missions and have made several trips with Towering Oaks and First Baptist Church to Louisiana and Mississippi after Hurricane Katrina. Rita also went to Belize with Towering Oaks mission team in March 2005. Jim and Rita plan on more activity in the mission field as they approach their retirement years. Both are also members of the Tennessee Disaster Relief Team.

Rita often speaks on behalf of Holston Methodist Children's Home, the place God chose to place her through his "divine intervention," a place where she found support, unconditional love, and eventually lived the benefits of planted seeds that were placed by those who cared and wanted to make a difference, which, she will add, they did. She has spoken at the Annual Holston United Methodist Conference at Lake Junaluska in North Carolina in 2005 to a crowd of twenty-five hundred persons. There Rita shared the benefits of Holston Methodist Children's Home for hurting and lonely lives. The speech ended with a standing ovation, *only* because the crowd was given a glimpse of a life victorious and the hand their support played in that victory. She has spoken at women's conferences as well as churches, where she also shares what their offerings do to benefit parentless, hurting children, again using her own life as an example.

Rita and Jim circle not just blood relatives in their lives but any and all who wish to be a part of their big, extended family. No one is a stranger to them or their home. After all, that was something Rita, at the ripe young age of fourteen, learned when her world changed as she entered a town unfamiliar and into a children's home as "one alone." Years later, she has a family which numbers many.

I have so many people to thank—people who have truly cared about me but I haven't mentioned. My sweet Judy, you are one I truly admire, I love you like a sister, just like I do Wendy. Tammy M., Velma, Pam and Frankie, Debbie and Bob, Ann W. Thank you, Ann, for always believing I was a good mother. My Sunday school class at Towering Oaks; my two church families, Towering Oaks and First Baptist Church. All of you have taught me true love. I also thank all of Jim's family of friends for caring about and accepting me. Blessings to all.